Chorus insignis monasterij Occidentalis.

excipitur

Variæ per orbem jubilatio

nouem

Innumera nobilium, aulicorum, et satellitum ante fores templi commorantium turba

KING JAMES

God gives not Kings the style of Gods in vain,
For on his throne his Sceptre do they sway:
And as their subjects ought them to obey,
So Kings should fear and serve their God again.

King James, *Basilikon Doron*

VI OF SCOTLAND
KING JAMES
I OF ENGLAND

Antonia Fraser

Alfred A. Knopf

New York 1975

Also by Antonia Fraser
Mary Queen of Scots
Cromwell: The Lord Protector

This is a Borzoi Book
published in New York by Alfred A. Knopf, Inc.

Copyright © 1974 by Antonia Fraser

All rights reserved under International and
Pan-American Copyright Conventions. Published
in the United States by Alfred A. Knopf, Inc., New
York. Distributed by Random House, Inc.,
New York. Originally published in Great Britain by
George Weidenfeld and Nicolson, London.

Library of Congress Catalog Card Number: 74–6150
ISBN: 0–394–49476–8

Printed in Great Britain

First American Edition

Contents

For my father Frank Longford
Beati Pacifici

Introduction

JAMES VI AND I, the King who united in his person the crowns of Scotland and England, has received a censorious press. Faults – and he was very far from faultless – have been given maximum treatment and virtues – which he did not lack – have been dismissed as being on a lesser scale. The result is that he has been derided for his failures, but not sufficiently praised for those instances where his judgment was in advance of his age, as for example in his desire for a proper union of England and Scotland, or his genuine and far-sighted love of peace. His contribution as a skilful and tenacious King of Scotland – in many ways the most successful King Scotland ever had – is often ignored: while the legacy of problems he inherited in England is overlooked.

Perhaps King James's private life is responsible for the tone of moral disapproval which is sometimes applied to him. Certainly he should not be defended, particularly in his later years, for the political powers allowed to a greedy favourite. But equally, this tone of moral disapproval should not be allowed to spread to other areas which were unaffected by his private life, just because his personal predilections followed a course outside the accepted norm. In popular esteem, James has been unfairly crushed between the image of successful majesty which is Queen Elizabeth and the image of democracy-on-the-march which is the English Civil War. Yet both these images owe something to fantasy.

James was not called the British Solomon in vain. His love of learning was genuine, deep-seated, and surely admirable by any standards except those of the most resolutely anti-intellectual Englishman. He presided over the age of Shakespeare's tragedies, John Donne, Webster, Ben Jonson, a not inappropriate figurehead in view of James's own intimate connection with that jewel of our literature, the Authorised Version of the Bible. As for the judgment attributed to King Henry IV of

France – 'the wisest fool in Christendom' – it is a seductive catchphrase; but like many such, it does more to conceal the truth than to reveal it. James was no fool, as his Scottish subjects discovered, even if he was not always wise.

During the preparation of this book, I have been much indebted to Christopher Falkus and Martha Caute, both of Weidenfeld and Nicolson, for editing and to Marcia Vale for picture research. As a biographical essay, it is obviously not intended to replace the previous full-length studies, or the recent collection of essays edited by Alan G. R. Smith, containing the most modern researches on the double reign. It is simply a plea for greater understanding and therefore greater sympathy for the first monarch of Great Britain, one who was, in the present writer's opinion, worthy of that great position.

Antonia Fraser

1 The Bairr

It is no matter of his tears, better that bairns should weep than bearded men.

The Master of Glamis about King James

PREVIOUS PAGES
The Darnley Memorial,
painted by Levinus de
Vogelaare. Before the
effigy of Lord Darnley
the infant James kneels in
prayer: 'Arise, O Lord,
and avenge the innocent
blood of the King.'
Behind him are his
grand-parents – Matthew,
Earl of Lennox, Margaret,
Countess of Lennox,
and his uncle, their son,
Charles Stuart. In the
corner is an inset picture
of the encounter at
Carberry Hill on 15 June
1567 when Mary Queen of
Scots surrendered to the
rebel lords.

OPPOSITE 'Queen Mary's
Room' in Edinburgh
Castle where James was
born on the morning of
19 June 1566. On the
ceiling are the royal
crowned monograms
M.R. and I.R. (Iacobus).
The coat-of-arms is that
of the House of Stuart.

JAMES STUART, THE SON of Mary Queen of Scots, was born on 19 June 1566 in Edinburgh Castle. The small cramped room in the south-east corner of the fortress can still be seen today, with the joint initials of mother and son on the ceiling. Blue taffeta had been commanded for the laying-in bed, ten ells of Holland for the cradle, and even the midwife received a grant of velvet for her dress. In spite of these precautions it was a difficult birth, and when the baby was finally born between ten and eleven in the morning he had a thin fine caul stretched over his face.

On the subject of her long ordeal Mary said afterwards that she had been so handled that she began to wish she had never been married. In fact, the Queen had a more serious motive to regret her marriage to her cousin Henry Stuart, Lord Darnley than the physical sufferings of childbirth. The royal couple who had produced James, glamorous, tall like gods as they might be, were by this point united only by their elegant physical appearance. James, their single offspring, came into an atmosphere of marital strife, murder, plot, counterplot, in which hints of his own illegitimacy seemed the least of his future troubles. The true bone of contention between James's parents was Darnley's position in relation to the Scottish Crown. Mary, having returned to Scotland a widow after the death of her first husband, Francis II, King of France, needed to marry again. She dallied with the idea of a number of suitable and unsuitable spouses before falling in love with her own cousin, son of the Earl and Countess of Lennox. Subsequently it proved to be a disastrous choice; but it was always likely to be a dangerous one, since Darnley, like Mary herself, had Tudor royal blood and thus lay within the line of succession to the English throne. Queen Elizabeth might well feel that Mary was deliberately bolstering up her own pretensions by such a union. Darnley was even an English subject – hence the Anglicised spelling of his family name compared to the Scottish spelling of Stewart. In the event, Elizabeth did make furious if fruitless attempts to veto the match beforehand.

However, had Darnley possessed attributes other than the long-legged good looks which had first attracted Mary, some benefits might still have come out of the marriage: Mary badly needed a stable support against her factious and often

RIGHT James VI at the age of eight; painting attributed to R. Lockey after Arnold van Brounckhorst.
FAR RIGHT Henry Stuart, Lord Darnley, with his younger brother Charles Stuart, Earl of Lennox; painting by Hans Eworth, 1563. The striking similarity between James and his father helps to disprove those theories which question his paternity.

THIS BE THE SONES OF H RIGHT HONERABLE FERLLE OF LENOXE AD
TE LADY MARGARETZ GRACE COVNTYES OF LENOXE AD ANGWYSE

1563

CHARLLES STEWARDE   HENRY STEWARDE LORD DAR
HIS BROTHER ÆTATIS 6   LEY AND DOWGLAS ÆTATIS 17

outright rebellious Scottish nobles. But Darnley proved to be both weak and vicious. And Mary's understandable refusal to make him co-ruler, as Francis had been, by granting him the Crown Matrimonial, provided an ideal opportunity for these same nobles to win Darnley to their cause. It was even suggested that Mary was enjoying a liaison with her Savoyard secretary David Riccio. The result was the savage butchery of the wretched servant at Holyrood in March 1566. Mary herself was condemned to watch it all: she was then six months pregnant with James. Darnley was also present, as one of the conspirators, and the barbarous nature of the slaying, deliberately done in the delicate Queen's presence, aroused still more horrid suspicions that her own death and that of the unborn child had also been intended. In the intricacies of the Scottish succession, Darnley was arguably his own wife's heir, if a Hamilton claim was dismissed as invalid (although any child born to Mary would inevitably have displaced the father); and if he had been acclaimed king by the support of the plotters after Mary's death, he would certainly have been in a strong position.

The shadow of the Riccio murder would continue to fall athwart the life of the young James for many a long year. For out of this sordid and ferocious crime emerged several elements which were to be of the greatest import in his early life. Firstly, Mary conceived an implacable aversion to her husband – for she at least was convinced that her death and that of the baby had been intended. With great self-control she concealed this aversion sufficiently to win Darnley away from his noble associates, and thereby escape from Holyrood in a desperate horseback flight to Dunbar. Her subsequent return to Edinburgh at the head of a more loyal group of nobles was in the nature of a triumph.

Secondly, the question of James's own paternity became involved in the murky circumstances of Riccio's death. If Mary had been Riccio's mistress, could not Riccio have been James's father? The story may be dismissed on its timing alone: James was conceived soon after Mary's marriage, at the height of her infatuation for Darnley. Equally far-fetched is the legend that James died at birth, and an Erskine baby, son of the Earl of Mar, was substituted – a story based on the discovery of some

OPPOSITE Mary Queen of Scots 'En Deuil Blanc' by an unknown artist, after the portrait by Francis Clouet probably painted at the time of her mourning for her father-in-law, Henry II.

nameless bones, not necessarily those of a child, in the walls of Edinburgh Castle in the nineteenth century. But, in any case, a comparison of James's portrait as a child with that of his father as a young man conveys a startling resemblance. 'My lord, God has given you and me a son, begotten by none but you,' said Mary when she first showed the baby to Darnley, uncovering its face. Her version may be accepted, although her subsequent ominous prediction was perhaps less accurate : 'He is so much your own son, that I fear it will be the worse for him hereafter.' Nevertheless the pettily vicious rumour continued to haunt James even in adulthood. Henry IV coined one of his unfair yet all too memorable aphorisms when he said that James was certainly the modern Solomon since he was the son of David (Riccio). It was a charge which reduced the grown man to fury, and on one occasion he wept with humiliation when the old scandal was revived in Scotland by his enemies.

The third effect of the Riccio murder was more prolonged. The preceding alliances of the ever feudacious Scottish nobles had been destroyed, not only by Mary's prompt escape, but also by the fact of Darnley's betrayal of their cause. The eight months between the birth of James and the death of his father at Kirk o'Field were therefore marked by new combinations in Scottish power politics. As Mary turned for support to the rugged but at least loyal Earl of Bothwell, other nobles who had been abandoned by Darnley considered his removal. Mary's half-brother, James, Earl of Moray, a prominent Protestant and much in touch with the English government, played a waiting-game. Mary tentatively explored the possibilities of a divorce or annulment, but faltered when it was explained to her that the legitimacy of James might be called in question.

It was in this atmosphere of mounting conflict and suspicion that the first months of James's life were lived. Indeed, the occasion of his christening on 17 December 1566 at Stirling Castle illustrated all too many of these tensions. The baptism was performed in the Chapel Royal according to the Catholic rite of James's mother. His father did not attend. On the one hand, the baby was carried to the font in the arms of the Count de Brienne, proxy for his godfather the King of France. On the other hand, the representative of Queen Elizabeth, the child's godmother, lurked outside the Catholic chapel like a bad fairy

to signify the firm Protestantism of her mistress. Yet the choice of the two sovereigns as sponsors showed that Mary hoped to enjoy both the support of Catholic France, and the ultimate royal reversion of Protestant England. In the meantime the magnificent gifts, a vast gold font from the English Queen, a bejewelled and feathered fan from the Duke of Savoy, a necklace of pearls and rubies from the King of France, signified, as did the rows of flaring torches and the proud presence of Mary's Catholic nobles, the last ceremonial occasion in the brief personal rule of Mary Stuart.

The culmination of the Scottish political intrigues came on the night of 9 February 1567 when the house in which Darnley was recovering from some noxious disease (possibly syphilis) was blown up by gunpowder. He himself was strangled. It is not necessary here to try to unravel the full intricacies of this, one of the most complicated plots in our island history. It is sufficient to note that any number of the Scottish nobles had a motive for wishing to be rid of Darnley, quite apart from Bothwell and Mary; prominent among them were the Earl of Morton, and his Douglas kinsmen. But from that point on, James's mother's fortunes ran rapidly downhill.

Stirling Castle where James was baptised on 17 December 1566. He spent most of the early years of his life at the castle under the guardianship of the Earl of Mar.

19

James Stewart, Earl of Moray, the first regent of Scotland during James's reign. He was assassinated at Linlithgow in 1570.

Whether Mary had foreknowledge of the murder or not – and with the exception of the highly dubious Casket Letters there is no contemporary evidence that she did – she behaved with exceptional imprudence thereafter. She married Bothwell, one of the chief suspects, only a little later. The intractable nobles were as ill-suited by the notion of Bothwell lording it over them as consort as they had been by that of Darnley. There were fresh alliances in view of the new common need to destroy Bothwell. Mary and her third husband were forcibly separated at Carberry Hill on 15 June 1567, never to meet again. The confederate lords' banner displayed the murdered corpse of Darnley and the child James praying 'Judge and defend my cause O Lord.' Mary, at the age of twenty-four, found herself incarcerated on the tiny island of Lochleven and obliged under duress to sign an Act of Abdication in favour of her son.

The new sovereign of Scotland, James, sixth of that name to reign over the country, was thirteen months old. He was crowned on 29 July 1567 in the Protestant church just outside the gates of Stirling Castle. In contrast to his Catholic christening, prayers on this occasion were said in 'the mother tongue', i.e. Scots. But the actual direction in which power had shifted was signified shortly afterwards when his uncle, the Earl of Moray, illegitimate son of James's grandfather, King James V, was made regent of the kingdom. It will be seen that even within the span of his short life, little James's person had been of much consequence, the subject of anxious debate. His birth had strengthened his mother's place in the English succession – a male heir was always a good card to possess, especially when confronting a Virgin Queen – and had in some manner freed her from the dynastic claims of Darnley. But James's existence had also fatally weakened Mary's hand in the alternative game she was compelled to play with her Scottish nobles. Who would not prefer a pliable infant sovereign, with the prospect of a long minority and profitable acquisitions coming the way of the nobles, to a spirited ruler? It was no coincidence that Mary, at the moment of her abdication, had been approaching her twenty-fifth birthday, the occasion on which she could have claimed back certain lands alienated during her own minority.

So began the reign of King James, born out of circumstances of storm and drama, the weakness of the Crown symbolised by the infant sovereign, the power of the nobles symbolised by his uncle's regency. Yet far from being a new phenomenon, a child monarch had become almost the norm in late mediaeval and Reformation Scotland. James's situation had many gloomy parallels with that of his royal forbears. Mary herself had become Queen when six days old, but there had been an earlier total of seven royal minorities with no adult succession since the fourteenth century. In battle and elsewhere, the Stewart Kings, having come precariously to manhood via disputed and contumacious regencies, in their manhood had fallen. The opportunities of the nobles to whittle away at the practical power of the Crown, as well as its landed and financial resources, had been limitless. Even the early history of the Stewarts served only to underline their essentially vulnerable position on the throne. As the name indicated, they had risen

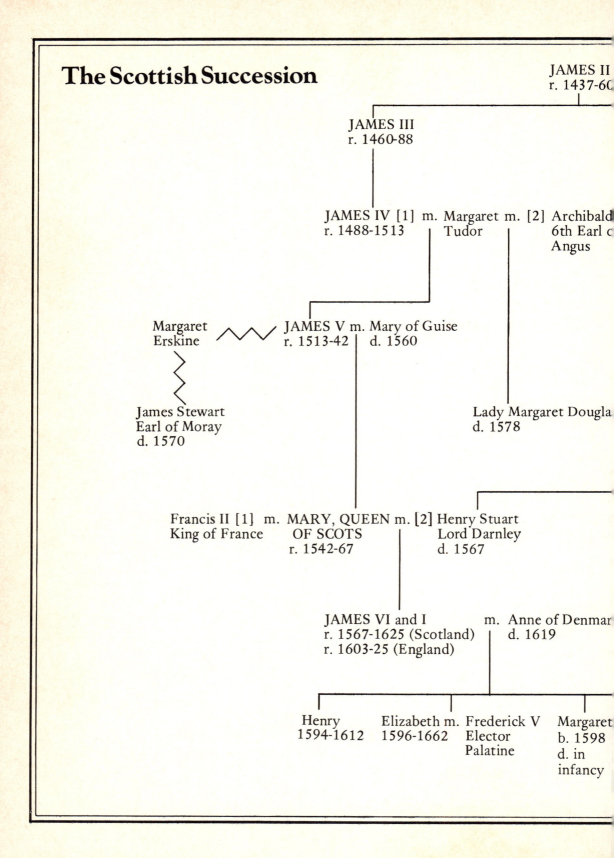

The Scottish Succession

JAMES II
r. 1437-60

JAMES III
r. 1460-88

JAMES IV [1] m. Margaret m. [2] Archibald
r. 1488-1513   Tudor   6th Earl c
                               Angus

Margaret
Erskine   JAMES V m. Mary of Guise
           r. 1513-42 d. 1560

James Stewart   Lady Margaret Dougla
Earl of Moray   d. 1578
d. 1570

Francis II [1] m. MARY, QUEEN m. [2] Henry Stuart
King of France   OF SCOTS   Lord Darnley
                  r. 1542-67   d. 1567

JAMES VI and I   m. Anne of Denmar
r. 1567-1625 (Scotland)   d. 1619
r. 1603-25 (England)

Henry   Elizabeth m. Frederick V   Margaret
1594-1612   1596-1662   Elector   b. 1598
                          Palatine   d. in
                                         infancy

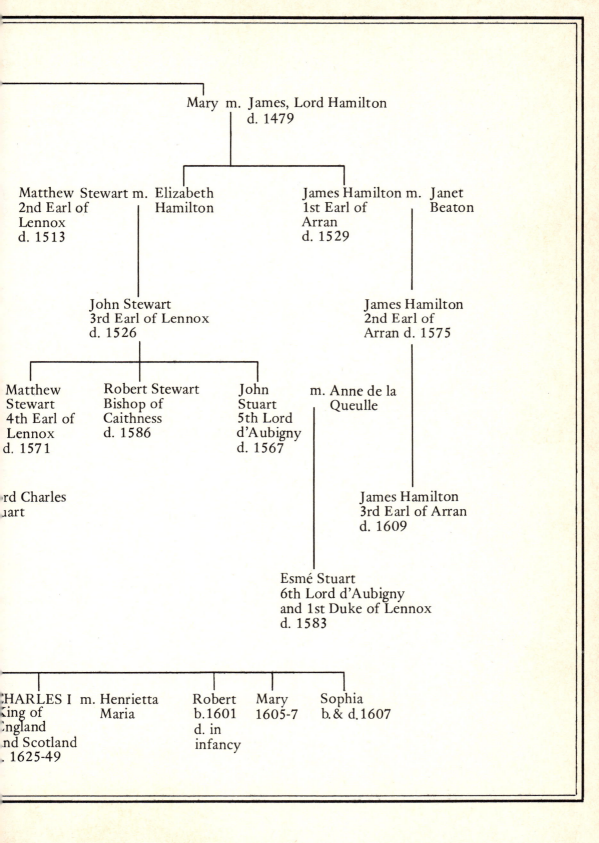

Mary m. James, Lord Hamilton
d. 1479

Matthew Stewart m. Elizabeth
2nd Earl of   Hamilton
Lennox
d. 1513

James Hamilton m. Janet
1st Earl of   Beaton
Arran
d. 1529

John Stewart
3rd Earl of Lennox
d. 1526

James Hamilton
2nd Earl of
Arran d. 1575

Matthew   Robert Stewart   John   m. Anne de la
Stewart   Bishop of   Stuart   Queulle
4th Earl of   Caithness   5th Lord
Lennox   d. 1586   d'Aubigny
d. 1571   d. 1567

rd Charles
uart

James Hamilton
3rd Earl of Arran
d. 1609

Esmé Stuart
6th Lord d'Aubigny
and 1st Duke of Lennox
d. 1583

CHARLES I m. Henrietta   Robert   Mary   Sophia
King of   Maria   b.1601   1605-7   b. & d.1607
England   d. in
nd Scotland   infancy
. 1625-49

from the position of royal stewards to that of sovereigns, via the marriage of Walter, sixth Great Steward, to Marjorie, daughter of Robert the Bruce. There was thus nothing sacrosanct and Ptolemaic about the Scottish Stewart monarchy whose origins were so well known.

A Stewart King was merely regarded as *primus inter pares*. Most of the nobility were in some way or other related to the monarchy, which did not increase their respect for it. The rich Earldom of Moray in the north-east had been granted to another Stewart, James's illegitimate uncle, the regent. The Earl of Lennox – James's grandfather – was another Stewart. The Erskine family were headed by the Earl of Mar, the traditional governor of an infant sovereign. There were many branches of the Douglas family (the Countess of Lennox had been a Douglas); one of these was headed by that Earl of Morton implicated in Darnley's murder. The relationship of these groups to each other and to the throne at any given moment is inevitably confusing: for they shifted perpetually, according to the dictates of territorial aggrandisement, religion or family alliance. In their own domains they enjoyed the advantages of a type of feudal jurisdiction, while the existence of their bands of family followers constituted a virtual standing army – something the sovereign did not have. At their best, these men had vigour and a capacity for survival. At their worst, they were capable of playing out power politics on a very rough scale indeed. At all times they surrounded the throne like wolves circling round a lone traveller, ever menacing, ever ready to pounce at a hint of weakness.

And causes of weakness, there could be only too many in the coming reign. Scotland was not a united nation religiously. The Act of Parliament which in 1560 had changed the official religion of the country to Protestantism ignored the fact that many of the population were still Catholics. In particular, the Catholic nobility soldiered on, encouraged by the rule of their co-religionist Mary: their possibilities of foreign intrigues would constitute a perpetual vexation to the adult James. As for those who professed the Reformed religion, divisions would begin to show between those who would now be termed Presbyterians and the Episcopalians who still supported their bishops. Religious differences apart, there were Scotland's economic difficulties. The Scottish Crown was woefully short of funds, and as such incapable of mustering such luxuries as a standing army, or indeed any proper armed force at all, except by virtue of the nobles' cooperation. The fact that its properties had been much alienated not only decreased the royal income, but also robbed the Crown of actual supporters.

In marked contrast to England, the Scottish Parliament was a negligible factor at this particular date. A single chamber, known as the Estates, its management was in the hands of a small body, the Lords of the Articles, who presented all business to it. Since the Lords of the Articles tended to represent whatever noble clique was in power, Parliament merely echoed this factious tendency. The system of Scottish land tenure at the moment of James's accession gave the Crown little proper chance to intervene between its tenants-in-chief and their tenants in matters of justice. Lower down the scale, there were of course the lairds, the lesser landed gentry who might prove possible allies in the future – but that would need organisation by a skilful central authority.

The country itself was poor, possessing a simple economy which could all too easily be upset by passing Acts of God, such as that ever present Scottish danger, a bad harvest. In many other respects Scotland in 1567 was a stark if powerfully beautiful country, barely emerged from the cocoon of a primitive way of life. There were fertile areas, it was true, such as the Kingdom of Fife on the east coast which James's grandmother Mary of Guise had tactfully admired on her arrival from France. But there were also vast tracts such as the Highlands or indeed the debateable Border country where it was difficult to know whose law obtained. This wildness was helped on by the fact that communications were lamentable; roads in general were so bad that it was hardly surprising that the first coach had been introduced to Scotland (from France) only five years before James's birth. Travellers and other representatives of the unfamiliar were generally disliked. The inevitable consequence of distance and poverty was attachment to the local magnate as provider rather than to the Crown as the central element in the State.

It may well be asked what hope there was for a small child brought up in this unwelcoming wasps' nest from babyhood.

From such a disadvantaged beginning, how could James hope to do better than the early deaths of his male ancestors, the dramatic failure of his beautiful mother? The extraordinary story of King James in Scotland is that he did do better, he did learn to cope in some manner or other with problems not long before apparently demonstrated to be insoluble. For an explanation of the surprising courage, competence and resourcefulness which this son of the unstable Mary and the feeble Darnley displayed, it is necessary to delve into his pathetic, bleak, but ultimately highly instructive childhood.

It is important to note that the first thirty-six years of James's life, with the exception of one short expedition to Scandinavia, were to be spent in Scotland. It was Scotland that was to form James, to twist him, if twisted he would be, or mould him successfully. Unlike his mother, whose dominant upbringing was in France, or his father, brought up in England, James was the nursling of the country of which he was the King. By the standards of the European royalty of the time, so often polyglot, James's blood also contained a peculiarly high proportion of Scots – nearly half. If we look at his grand-parents, we find that Darnley's father was Scottish and his mother Lady Margaret Douglas, half-Scottish and half-English. Mary's father, Margaret's step-brother, was equally half-Scots and half-English; Mary's mother was French. By marrying each other, Mary and Darnley, who were step-first cousins, thus produced a child whose Scottish noble ancestry was noticeably predominant.

The first stages of James's childhood were scarcely more serene than his infancy. In May 1568 Mary escaped from her island prison of Lochleven; but almost immediately her supporters were crushed at the battle of Langside. She fled to England, seeking help from Elizabeth, only to find herself once more incarcerated. Thus while Mary languished in a series of English prisons, the regent Moray ruled in his nephew's name until his own assassination in 1570. Thereafter the regency passed to James's paternal grandfather, the Earl of Lennox, the choice incidentally of the English Queen. But the Marians, who from a variety of motives, continued to appeal to England for the restoration of James's mother, did not give in without a struggle. A type of civil war broke out. Lennox himself died

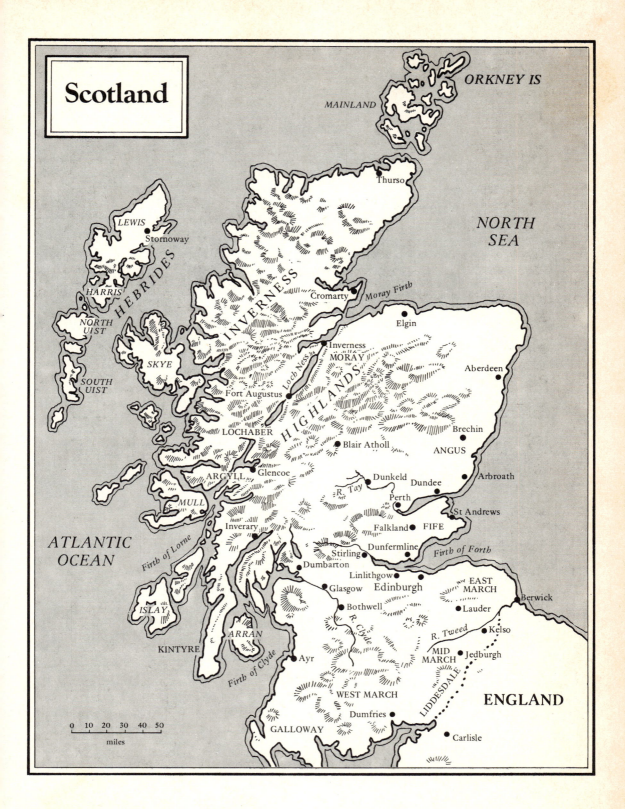

James Douglas, Earl of Morton, the fourth and last regent during James's reign. Morton was executed in 1581 for the crime of having contrived the murder of Darnley.

in a foray in September 1571, his mortally wounded body, with its life ebbing away, actually passing under the appalled gaze of his little grandson – and James had been very fond of Lennox. Then the Earl of Mar succeeded as regent until his own death, almost surprisingly from natural causes. It was then the turn of the Earl of Morton, who from 1573 onwards, by a judicious mixture of strength and ruthlessness, did for a time put an end to the plague of skirmishes, civil and military, which had been raging virtually since James's accession.

When Morton assumed power, the boy King was almost seven years old. He had known but little of emotional stability which is nowadays considered so important to the happy development of a child. He last saw his mother when he

was under a year old, and could therefore retain absolutely no memory of her in later years (in contrast to the wretched Mary who treasured her own memories of her baby in captivity, ignoring the fact that her baby had grown up into an unknown young man). Even before their separation, James, as was traditional with the Princes of Scotland, had been given to the governorship of the Earl of Mar and his wife. It was therefore the Mars who in household terms exercised the formative pressures upon James as a boy. It was a matter of further bad luck, then, that to an absent mother and a dead father was added a harsh surrogate parent. Lady Mar was extremely strict in her notions of upbringing, as a result of which, as contemporaries agreed, James was much in awe of her.

His material wants were not neglected: among the food provided there were certain rations 'for the King's mouth only'; there was a wet nurse when that was appropriate, and four young lady 'rockers' to cope with the problem of the royal cradle. Nevertheless it was more characteristic of James's upbringing that his bed was draped in sombre black damask, with pillows fringed in black. And when the time came for the education of the child – not yet four years old – to be arranged, the stern atmosphere was not alloyed. One of his tutors, Master Peter Young, had a kindly nature for which James was duly grateful, but there was not much gentleness to be expected from his senior tutor George Buchanan. A brilliant scholar and poet, Buchanan was also the most venomous of Mary's traducers and it was his work listing her supposed crimes which constituted the body of charges against her at the time. In addition, Buchanan was now old, crabbed, and for all his scholarly attainments, capable of 'extremely vengeable' behaviour to those who offended him. There are certainly stories that he exacted this vengeance against the son of Mary Queen of Scots when the child crossed him, calling him the true bird of the blood nest from which he sprang.

In one way, Buchanan did his work well. James's formidable learning, which was to make him the amused wonder of the cynical western world, is attested by his library, full of Greek and Latin books grafted on to the French romances left behind by his mother. Peter Young described a typical day in his studies, starting with prayers to propitiate the deity, then Greek – the New Testament, Isocrates or Plutarch. After breakfast, came Latin – Livy, Justin or Cicero; after dinner, composition, and then arithmetic or cosmography, which included geography and astronomy, or dialectics or rhetoric. It was no wonder that primed with such learning, by the age of eight, James was marching up and down, holding Lady Mar's hand and astonishing an observer by discoursing on knowledge and ignorance. He could also perform such useful feats as translating aloud a chapter of the Bible from Latin into French and then into English.

The religious education of the young King was naturally not neglected. Although for organisational reasons James would later turn away from Presbyterianism to a type of Episcopalianism and later Anglicanism, it was in the severe Calvinist-inspired

lady minny this is to schaw you that I haue re-
ceiuit your fruite & thankes you theifoire
is readie for mee quhen ye pleis to send theme
& sall gif as few by me as I may. & I will
not trouble you farther quhill meting quho
sall be as sconlie as I may god willing. and
sa fair ye weill as I do thks to god.

James R

Sir Peter Young, tutor to
the young James. A kindly
man, he won the boy's
affection and became a
favourite counsellor. He
accompanied James to
London in 1603 and
became a tutor to Prince
Charles in 1604.

George Buchanan, the
greatest of the Scottish
humanists in the sixteenth
century, and James's
senior tutor from 1570 to
1578.

James's signature in his exercise book in Latin, French and English.

form of the Scottish Protestant Church that he was nutured. And James continued to cast a friendly eye towards Calvinist theology, long after he had rejected the political consequences of Presbyterianism. Just as he was constantly told by Buchanan that his mother had been an adulteress and a murderess (a view he subsequently angrily rejected), he was also imbued with those notions of divine retribution, the distinction between the saved and the non-saved, the importance of grace, that characterised this dour yet forceful religion. As a result, James retained all his life an enormous and energetic interest in all forms of theological discussion and dispute, which quite apart from his intellectual pursuits sets him apart from other British sovereigns.

Nor was the body of the new Solomon neglected in all this, though compared to the intellect it was poor material to work upon. Physically, James never measured up to his parents: the critical conditions of his birth, and that fierce ante-natal experience of the midnight horseride to Dunbar, had probably seen to that. From his father he inherited his hair, thick and fair in childhood, darkening to light brown in later years, and those sad heavy-lidded eyes, which when passed on to his own son Charles I, were to become famous in our portraiture as the hall-mark of a Martyr King. From Mary, James inherited not the fatal beauty, but the long nose and small mouth, in his case suspiciously cast down and tucked in at the corners. Yet although James had not inherited his parents' exceptional height, it would be wrong to think of him, as his enemies and the satirists did, as being exceptionally small. Impartial contemporary accounts unite in referring to him as being of middle height. With his broad shoulders and bent legs (he did suffer from

33

rickets acquired in childhood) which made his steps uneven and erratic, he was somewhat tadpole-shaped; but he was certainly not grossly deformed, beyond the weakness of one foot turned permanently outwards. Like all the Stuarts, James was a fanatic for physical exercise. Perhaps hunting, his favourite sport, freed him from the restrictions of his body; on horseback the ungainly youth became a fleet-footed centaur.

For all the dancing of his childhood, a necessary courtly practice, and possibly golf (there is definite evidence that Mary Queen of Scots played, and James in his turn received presents of 'two golfe clubbes'), the result of this arid

A sixteenth-century painting of a young golf player. Golf was a popular game in Scotland by the mid-fifteenth century and was known from early times as 'the royal game' James, like his mother Mary, certainly took an interest in the sport and received presents of 'golfe clubbes'.

One of the earliest gold coins issued during the reign of James VI, dated 1576. The over large sword contrasts with the frail figure of the boy king.

concentrated upbringing was to produce what was in effect a little old man. A coin of the period displays the pathetic sight of the slight boy King armed with an enormous sword, a weapon from which the pacific James would have flinched in real life. It illustrates the contrast between his magnificent theoretical position and his tutored practical present.

But James also derived other qualities from his education, two of which were to stand him in good stead. The first of these and the most important was a deep and canny reserve, the ability to keep his own counsel and form his own judgments without necessarily sharing them immediately, which it is impossible not to see as a direct result of his traumatic upbringing. Second was a wry sense of humour, the original pawky wit of the Scots, which one glimpses quite early on in his life – as, for example, when he scrawled in his books that he had been made to speak Latin before he could speak Scots. Aged five, when he was taken into Parliament at a critical moment in the struggles of his grandfather with the

35

nobility, James found a tattered table-cloth and observed: 'This Parliament hath a hole in it.' A tyrant, said James, was *tir ane* in Scots, to strip one of one's property. *'Un prêtre'* was rightly so called because he was *'prête* [ready] *à malfaire'*. He was told that as King he should never be angry, to which James replied, referring to the Lion of Scotland on his crest: 'Then I should not wear the lion in my arms, but rather a sheep.' One admires the youthful pluck which dragged out of the constricted childhood this capacity for jokes. Later in adulthood, James had a knack of delivering his jests 'in a grave and serious manner' which is characteristic of the most successful comedians.

But there was a third dominant quality which James derived from this loveless if educative background which would not prove so fortunate. That was an inability to resist love when it was offered to him, because he had been so starved of early affection. James grew up with a passionate desire to love and to be loved in the romantic sense, to worship something beyond himself, something fairer, more physically perfect than the stunted prodigy's body with which he had been endowed. It is a quality for which James has been harshly judged, for the simple reason that the first love object which came his way was a man. But one can at least advance the opinion that had an equally attractive woman come his way at the same propitious moment, the homosexual inclinations of King James might never have been aroused.

The man in question, Esmé Stuart Sieur d'Aubigny, a French connection of the royal Stewarts, arrived at a crucial moment during the King's adolescence. The brief period of solidarity under Morton's regency had given way in its turn before the eternal feuds to which the Scots were so subject. The premise that the Scottish nation was ungovernable by one single agency seemed thereby to have received further confirmation. In the bickering which followed – although that is perhaps too mild a word – between Morton, the young Earl of Mar, and his uncle Alexander Erskine who had succeeded as James's governor, the custody of James remained of prime importance as indeed it had been since his birth. In these difficult years, James's actual person never ceased to be the bone over which these aggressive dogs snapped and quarrelled, and that in itself must have been a terrifying experience for a timid friendless boy.

36

It was in September 1579, shortly after James's thirteenth birthday, that Esmé Stuart arrived from France. His original motivation is slightly obscure but it seems that he was an emissary from Mary's French relations, the Catholic Guises. On arrival in Scotland he rapidly deserted their cause – and hers – for the more profitable relationship with the King. He certainly announced himself a convert to Protestantism. And there was no question that the touchingly love-deprived adolescent boy did fall violently in love with his elegant and attainable older cousin. Stuart's looks, with his aristocratic high cheek-boned face and fine straight nose, survive the fashions in portraiture to make one understand James's admiration. In addition, Esmé Stuart had that lightness of touch, that glamour, from his French upbringing which had so long ago gilded James's mother Mary, but which he himself so singularly lacked. In essence it was a romantic passion, although there seems no reason to suppose that it was not also consummated, thus setting James firmly in the pattern where he associated sexual love with men. To James it seemed that paradise had come on earth when this beloved god, this Phoenix as he termed him in one of his own poems, actually returned his affections.

Drawing of Esmé Stuart, James's first favourite.

As affection of course it was not only unnatural as far as the outside world was concerned, but also doomed in political terms, since Esmé Stuart determined to take advantage of the association. He rose rapidly to the position of Duke of Lennox, with accompaniments of rich gifts such as the Abbey of Arbroath and the custody of Dumbarton Castle. Lennox's boon companion, the far more disreputable and less attractive James Stewart, was created Earl of Arran. Together the unholy pair plotted that Morton should be arrested and tried on the ancient charge of the murder of Darnley. For this he was ultimately executed in 1581.

If the ghost of Darnley was laid, the person of the King was far from being secure against further assaults. On the contrary, the death of Morton merely marked another period in which the dogs quarrelled angrily over their royal bone. The Scottish Presbyterian ministers and their supporters among the nobles viewed the triumvirate of Lennox, Arran and the young James with no enthusiasm, especially as Lennox encouraged James in the view that the ministers were seeking to encroach on his position as King. Was this situation to be endured? In Scotland, the answer was most emphatically that it was not. The test case came over the appointment of one Robert Montgomery to the bishopric of Glasgow, a choice thoroughly unacceptable to the Presbyterian General Assembly, headed by the formidable Andrew Melville. The upshot of the dissensions was once more physical retribution directed against James. In the famous Raid of Ruthven of 22 August 1582, the Earl of Gowrie, head of the house of Ruthven and a prominent Ultra-Protestant, kidnapped the King.

Poor James, humiliated, wretched, forsaken and lovesick, was nevertheless forced to issue a proclamation against Lennox and Arran. The King's 'grief of mind' was terrible. A torrent of tears greeted the implacable demands of the Ruthvens to which the Master of Glamis, another leading Protestant, merely said grimly that it was no matter of James's tears since it was 'better that bairns should weep than bearded men'. 'Which words,' commented an observer, 'entered so deeply into the King's heart, as he did never forget them.' Nevertheless to France went Lennox, leaving James to write the most poignant of all his youthful poems on the subject of his Phoenix; his 'Fowl of light':

> And shall I then like bird or beast forget
> For any storms that threatening heaven can send
> The object sweet, where'on my heart is set
> Whom for to serve my senses all I bend?...

Doubtless it is true, as Andrew Melville angrily put it, that in one sense Lennox had held the King 'in a misty night of captivity and black darkness of shameful servitude', or as Calderwood wrote, those twin debauchees, Lennox and Arran, had 'foully misused his tender age'. But it is important to realise that the real objections to Lennox were on the political level. Power in Scotland was ever in contest, and few who possessed it during this period survived long to enjoy it. In the meantime, the psychological effect on James of this cruel blighting of his youthful affections may be imagined. Perhaps first love is rarely destined to end happily, but few experiences can have ended as desolately as that of James Stuart. Today, when we contemplate his subsequent search to recapture the golden youthful quality of his early passion, we can see in it something at least which was as much pathetic as unwise.

If James had learnt one lesson during his appalling upbringing, it was expressed in the words of his own verse, written when he was fifteen years old:

> Since thought is free, think what thou will
> O troubled heart to ease thy pain
> Thought unrevealed can do no ill
> But words past out turn not again
> Be careful, aye, for to invent
> The way to get thine own intent ...
> With patience then see thou attend
> And hope to vanquish at the end.

It was time to see how – and if – that vanquishing could be achieved. For the parlous conditions brought about by the Raid of Ruthven were shortly to be reversed. A conservative reaction, with the help of lords such as Huntly, Crawford, Argyll and Rothes, unsaddled the Ruthven extremists. The King was rescued from the Raiders. Although Lennox was not returned to him, James was at least saved from the Ultra-Protestants, and Arran was soon a member of his Council once more. In June 1583, at the age of seventeen, James was now in theory at least of an age to assume the full government of Scotland, thrust into his tiny hands so many years before in the tiny hillside church at Stirling.

The Lennox Jewel, once thought to commemorate James's grandfather's death in 1571. It is now suggested that it may date from the period of Mary's marriage to Darnley.

39

2

Ye Highlands and Ye Lowlands

Ye Highlands and Ye Lowlands,
O where hae ye been?
They hae slain the Earl of Moray
And hae laid him on the green.

Ballad of the Bonnie Earl of Moray

A NUMBER OF PROBLEMS faced King James on his formal assumption of power. Not all of these were contained within the boundaries of Scotland. England had also to be considered, partly in terms of his cousin Elizabeth, still without a formal successor to her throne. Then there was his mother, still languishing there as a captive: Queen Mary had by no means abandoned the prospect of her rescue, either by the hands of foreign Catholics, or more fittingly from a son to a mother, by the hands of James. It was this maternal optimism which led to her abortive attempt from 1582 onwards to form an 'Association' for the joint rule of herself and James – a project which naturally envisaged her own return to Scotland. As her part of the bargain, Mary offered her acknowledgment of James's Kingship of Scotland, which she had never done previously, maintaining with truth that the Act of Abdication had been signed under duress at Lochleven. Their mutual letters indicated the fumbling nature of the confusion, for James addressed his mother as Queen of Scots, but signed himself James R. And in two ways James would have been happy to have seen this muddle eliminated: firstly, it would have helped him when dealing with the Catholic powers such as France and Spain; secondly, it would conceivably be of aid in the vexed matter of the English succession.

The clever if cold-hearted manner in which James handled these delicate negotiations was the first public indication of the strange resources with which his childhood had endowed him. It is pointless to blame James for the lack of emotion, the mature cunning, which he displayed in handling his absent and unknown mother: their cut-off had been complete, and even the toys such as little gold guns which Mary had lovingly despatched from captivity to Scotland had never reached their destination. Mary's emissary, Fontenay, in August 1584 was astonished that James asked him no questions about his mother, 'neither of her health, nor of the way she is treated, nor of her servants, nor what she eats or drinks, nor of her recreation, nor any similar matter'. Notwithstanding this blankness, Fontenay was convinced that James loved Mary with all his heart. Fontenay's powers of observation were better than his judgment. James, as so often in his life, would make a cerebral assessment concerning his mother. He would deride his former

PREVIOUS PAGES
Hawking scene from Turberville's *The Noble Art of Hunting,* 1578.

OPPOSITE A letter from James to his mother, written when he was twelve years old and signed by his tutor Buchanan.

42

Traist freind we greit zow weill Vpoun the knawlege had be
ws of the convening of sum of oure nobilitie and vtheris in armes appearandlie
to trouble the quiet estate we haif takin occasioun to wryte to zow and
vtheris oure trusty subiectis desiring zow effectuuslie that ze
faill not with zoure freindis servandis and dependaris weill bodin in
feir of weir to be at ws heir with all possible diligence prepairit
to remane and serve as ze salbe commandit for the space of [illegible] dayis
as ze will declair zoure gude affectioun to oure service and do ws
plesour Thus we commit zow to God From oure castell of
Striviling the [illegible] day of July 1578

James R

G Buchanan

tutor Buchanan for his lies about Mary in the *Detection*, instruct Camden in England to give her due honour for her sufferings, and in his own *Basilikon Doron* take care to castigate Moray for his unnatural rebellion. But love, his heart – these things were simply not in James's power to give.

It was not helpful to Mary that her messenger to the Scottish Court, the young and beautiful Master of Gray, quickly saw where the power lay and allied himself secretly with James. Similarly James played Mary along, until it became obvious that he had far more to gain from the goodwill – and the coffers – of Queen Elizabeth, than from any 'Association' with his mother. Finally James made a public demonstration of the switch in March 1585 when it was formally concluded by his Council that 'the Association desired by his mother should neither be granted nor spoken of hereafter'. Mary, broken-hearted, might rage and cry at the impiety and ingratitude of 'her child', but there is no doubt that James emerged from these intrigues with his hand greatly strengthened in that direction where his eyes were now cast so lovingly, the kingdom of Elizabeth. The English Queen sent an emissary offering £4,000 down, and £4,000 yearly, and in July 1586 an agreement was made along these lines.

James's Scottish problems were in the first instance religious, with that of the nobility not far behind. In any case the two ran into each other as the religious alliances of respective lords inevitably affected their political allegiances. One of the difficulties of the Reformed Church in Scotland was that the Act of 1560, which formally established Protestantism, had not solved the problem of church endowment, or indeed of ecclesiastical administration. At a local level the Protestant Church or Kirk was run by the ministers; then at national level there was the General Assembly. But it was not clear at first what if anything was to lie in between; the First Book of Discipline of 1561 had allowed a limited form of episcopacy in the shape of 'superintendents'. During James's minority, the Convention of Leith of 1572 had gone further and re-established the hierarchy although in a limited form. In the meantime there were those, principal amongst them the ecclesiastical leader Andrew Melville, who believed passionately that the Scottish Church should follow a true Presbyterian model – without bishops. It

44

The inscriptions on the painting read:

...D·GRATIA / ...SCOTORV / ...SVÆ 40

1583

IACOBVS / DEI·GRATIA / REX·SCOTOR / ÆTATIS·SVÆ

is Melville who has been described as 'the real founder of Scottish Presbyterianism'.

Naturally the position of the monarchy was affected by these struggles, even if the situation in James's youth was not quite so clear-cut as he later expressed it in his classic watchword: 'No Bishop, No King'. But Melville did believe passionately in the supremacy of Presbytery and its ministers. The Second Book of Discipline of 1581, adopted by the General Assembly if not by the government, swept away every trace of episcopacy. Undoubtedly, had Melville been allowed to have his way unchecked, a clerical oligarchy would have ensued; for although

An imaginary portrait of James with his mother, Mary Queen of Scots, painted in 1583 by an unknown artist. They never in fact met after 1567.

Melville preached the doctrines of the Two Kingdoms, spiritual and state, he firmly suggested that it was the Church's business in all this to 'teach the magistrate', i.e. James, rather than the other way round.

However, Scottish Presbyterianism was not in fact allowed to grow rampantly. In 1584, after a struggle which had been continuing since the fall of Morton, the King's position was actually reaffirmed as head of the Church. The influence of Patrick Adamson, Archbishop of St Andrews and a keen supporter of Episcopalianism, ascended and that of the Presbyterian faction diminished. Melville was summoned to stand trial for seditious preaching and fled to England. The so-called 'Black Acts' of May 1584 castigated 'the new pretended presbyteries' while supporting the King's ecclesiastical authority and reaffirming that of the bishops. As a result, the most violent of the ministers were compelled to depart. The re-establishment of Episcopalianism had the good effect of preventing the King from falling totally under the control of the rigid Ultra-Protestant clique, a position which would hardly have suited his growing theories of monarchical authority. At the same time it did not materially disrupt the social fabric of Scotland : the return of the bishops did not inhibit the sessions of the Kirk lower down from continuing to operate undisturbed. There was thus a distinct possibility that both Ultra-Protestants and Episcopalians could be able to function together.

James displayed the same pragmatism over the problem of the nobility. As with religious differences, he had sufficient acumen to understand that while it was not within his scope to reconcile the theoretical aims of all the warring noble factions, it might be possible to reconcile their practical intentions. When the extremist lords, exiled after the upsetting of the Ruthven *coup,* were returned by Elizabeth to Scotland, Arran in turn found his power challenged. James had no choice but to surrender Arran as his Chancellor and Arran, as Lennox had once been obliged to do, fled. The Protestant lords were back in charge. But from James's point of view, the important fact was that the King's authority still bobbed bravely on the turbulent waves of the nobles' disagreements. Although little proper peace could be expected between the rival claims of the conservative lords in the north headed by the Catholic Huntly, and the totally opposed Ultra-Protestant faction, at least the waves did not quite close over James's head. He was obliged to pardon the exiled lords, since in terms of power politics he had little other choice, but he did have the spirit to compel them to kneel down before him, as though he was King in more than name. According to Melville, he spoke to them 'pertly and boastingly as though he had been victorious over them, calling them traitors'.

The first great test of the new Anglo-Scottish *rapprochement,* of which the formal expression had been signed in July 1586, occurred over the death of James's mother in 1587. Once again, James showed a nice – if that is the right word – sense of proprieties. Through the twists and turns of intrigue, negotiation and public protest, it is clear that his position in the English succession took ultimate precedence over all other considerations. In the limbo period between Mary's trial and execution, it seems likely that one of his agents was given secret instructions to make it clear to Elizabeth that James, although concerned, would not in the end sacrifice the English alliance in order to stay the supreme sentence. James's reaction to his mother's actual death, on 8 February 1587, was equally ambivalent. According to one story, he observed gleefully 'Now I am sole King'; according to another, he went to bed sorrowfully without eating; according to a third, his countenance remained impassive at the news. In psychological terms, the last account seems the most plausible. The martial spirit of the noble who appeared before him in armour, saying that this was the proper mourning for a Queen of Scotland, was singularly lacking from the cautious wary character of the dead woman's son.

In view of the perilous existence to which any Scottish monarch was condemned, it is pleasant to record that the young King did create some diversions for himself. He formed round him a cultivated circle of poets and other *litterateurs,* reflecting his own interests. There was Alexander Montgomerie, given the title of James's 'master poet', the musicians Thomas and Robert Hudson, and William Fowler, uncle of the poet William Drummond of Hawthornden. As for James's own poetic efforts, while never in the class of brilliance, some of them, later revised and published as juvenilia, were curiously touching and effective. In England, where they made some impact, Sir

Philip Sidney referred to James's patronage of Christian verse. It is true that a note of bathos crept in from time to time, notably in his poem *Lepanto* :

> My pen for pity cannot write
> My hair for horror stands
> To think how many Christians there
> Were killed by pagan hands ...

But occasional bathos is a trap into which many amateur poets have fallen. James retained throughout his life a preoccupation with the subject of verse, particularly the mechanics of it all. The point about his literary interests was that they were transparently sincere, a virtue sometimes missed in the accusations of plagiarism. Plagiarism is the temptation of the royal patron, and to that temptation James succumbed, as also to the parallel lure of allowing the ready pens of his *protegés* to supplement his own. Nevertheless it was much to his credit that an atmosphere so conducive to the well-being of literature was introduced at the Scottish Court.

Apart from his own works, James showed a felicitous taste in encouraging others to write projects – this disposition, which would pay such magnificent dividends in the commissioning of the English Bible, was already discernible in Scotland. Thomas Hudson was challenged to translate Du Bartas's *Historie of Judith*, since James had given the opinion during a dinner-table conversation that the French of Du Bartas was inimitable in English. In his introduction Hudson courteously acknowledged that the finished result had been corrected by James's own hand. James's own juvenilia, somewhat revised from early versions, were published in *Essayes of a Prentise in the Divine Art of Poesie* of 1584 and *His Majesties Poeticall Exercises at Vacant Houres* of 1591.

The various character sketches of James in his young manhood are curiously contradictory. On the one hand, he judged wisely, had a retentive memory, understood matters clearly, asked keen and penetrating questions, and gave sound replies. 'In any argument, whatever it is about, he maintains the view that appears to him most just and I have heard him support Catholic against Protestant opinions. ...', wrote one observer. On the other hand, he was 'too given to pleasure, allowing all business to be conducted by others'. In England, this mixture of

OPPOSITE The execution of Mary Queen of Scots at Fotheringhay Castle on 8 February 1587.

49

Of the Hunt, and how he ought to dreſſe, gouerne, and attend his dogges.   Chap. 13.

A Good keeper of hounds ſhould be gratious, curteous, and gentle, louing his dogs of a naturall diſpoſition, and he ought to be both well footed and well winded, aſwell to fill his horne as his bottell: the firſt thing which he ought to do when he riſeth, is to go ſée his hounds, to make their lodging cleane, and to dreſſe thé as the caſe ſhall require: after he hath ſo clenſed them, he ought to take his horne and ſound thrée or foure times

Hunting was one of James's favourite pastimes and he pursued the sport enthusiastically in Scotland and England.
LEFT An illustration from Turberville's *The Noble Art of Hunting* shows a keeper with his hound.
OPPOSITE Engraving of a falconer by Jost Amman.

self-confidence and self-indulgence might not meet with such happy results. But one is obliged to admit that in Scotland his pleasures probably enabled James to survive what was otherwise a fairly unendurable existence. It was just as well for him that he had that lively, vital quality noted by a Jesuit in 1580, which made him 'not melancholy but sanguine' and 'quick to laugh and talk'.

The thrill of the chase, the charm of the literary dinner table, these delights might have kept King James occupied for many years. But it was the duty of a king to seek a queen. There was no dynasty more aware of the perils of childlessness than the

51

Stuarts who had proved as a family singularly unfruitful. As a result, the Scottish family nearest to the throne, the Hamiltons, had for a hundred and fifty years stood virtually one heartbeat away from it. James applied himself with energy to the task of selecting a bride; he did not by nature particularly enjoy the company of women, despising their intelligence in principle along masculine chauvinistic lines, a point of view easy to hold in Scotland where women, although spirited, were not much educated. But a wife would be different. As James himself said with regard to his bachelorhood, 'this my nakedness made me to be weak and my enemies strong, and the want of succession bred disdain'.

James also had a streak of romance in his nature, and there is every reason to suppose that it was aroused initially by his eventual choice of a bride. This was Anne, the fourteen-year-old daughter of the King of Denmark. The story that King James prayed over her portrait together with that of Catherine of Bourbon for a fortnight is probably apocryphal: the lack of a Bourbon dowry doubtless clinched matters in favour of Anne. But it was James himself who took the chivalrous decision to venture to Scandinavia to meet her when she became marooned in Norway on her winter's journey to Scotland. They were Hero and Leander, he wrote (presumably he hoped for a better fate), and in another verse:

The seas are now the bar
Which make us distance far
That we may soon win near
God grant us grace.

When James arrived in Oslo, he found a typical Scandinavian beauty, golden-haired, white-skinned, in figure tall and slender; James's description of Anne's youthful appearance – 'our earthly Juno and our gracious queen' – seems peculiarly apt. Admittedly as James rushed excitedly into the Norwegian palace 'boots and all', the poor Princess's spirits faltered slightly. The young couple conversed nervously in French, while James was compelled to practise his excellent Latin on the Norwegians, who found themselves in the unexpected position of hosts to this royal romance. The wedding ceremony, performed then and there, was also marred by mishap: the four Negroes, commissioned by James to dance artistically in the snow, all subsequently perished of pneumonia.

But a positive idyll followed. James returned with his bride to her native Denmark and wintered there, or as James Melville put it, having travelled 'through many woods and wilderness, in the confined frost and snow … there made good cheer, and drank stoutly till spring time'. On their arrival back in Scotland on 1 May 1590, the chariot of the Queen was drawn by eight horses caparisoned in velvet, embroidered richly in silver and gold; the King rode before. During Anne's coronation procession the Mercat Cross of Edinburgh ran claret wine upon the causeway 'for the loyalty of that day'; the township presented the young Queen with a box covered in purple velvet, with an A for Anne on it in diamonds worth 20,000 crowns; lastly Anne encountered the Goddess of Corn and Wine, also sitting at the Mercat Cross with heaps of corn about her, who informed her in Latin that there should be plenty thereof in her time.

And plenty – or rather fertility – did attend upon the marriage. A quiverful of children followed: Henry, Elizabeth, Margaret, Charles, Robert, Mary and Sophia. Although only three of these survived to adulthood, Anne's strong Scandinavian blood had evidently thickened the febrile trickle of the Stuarts and the spectacle of a young family in the royal nursery was something which Scotland had not seen since far back in its history. Sophia, the youngest, buried in Westminster Abbey in a touching cradle-shaped tomb, was born and died in 1607, so that it will be seen that marital relations continued between James and Anne for at least sixteen years. In spite of their subsequent gradual parting, and for all the dour criticisms which have been made of Anne's frivolity, it is difficult not to conclude that James was fortunate in his selection. Emotionally, their first years together were marked by genuine love, which later gave place gracefully to a gentler sense of companionship. When James left for England, he wrote a tender letter to Anne, temporarily left behind, praying God to preserve her and 'all the bairns' and wishing for 'a blithe meeting' with her and a couple of them.

Anne had much natural royal graciousness as well as a comforting if unexciting niceness of character. Her lack of brains, her love of 'night-waking and balling' which caused grumbles

among the Scots, can scarcely have surprised her husband, who had been trained by Buchanan to have a quick eye for what he considered to be the weaknesses of femininity. He disliked painted faces, for example, and distrusted long hair as part of 'an alluring beauty' which boded no good for the male sex. It is true that Anne's conversion to Catholicism from her native Lutheranism would arouse suspicion and (groundless) fears concerning the education of her children. And in the past she has been much criticised by historians for her undue love of pleasure and her extravagance in pursuing it. However, since the fruits of this passion, such as her patronage of Inigo Jones, are so admirable in themselves, it is pleasant to find that in modern times Queen Anne has made up in the approval of art historians what she has lost in the disapproval of more political pundits. By the standards of princely couples then, James and Anne were certainly not flagrantly unhappy and they were blessed with a large family. In both respects they had the advantage of all James's immediate forbears and most of his Tudor cousins. As Bishop Goodman put it, 'they did love as well as man and wife could do, not conversing together.' It could even be said to have been a good – royal – marriage.

On James's return to Scotland, the immediate crisis which faced him was less cosy than the domesticity into which he was now plunged. To this period belongs the great witchcraft debate centring round the trials of the North Berwick witches on the south-east coast of Scotland, and the peculiar personality of Francis, Earl of Bothwell. The name Bothwell might well be considered fatal to the Stuarts: the Wizard Earl, as this Bothwell was known, was not actually descended from Mary's third husband, but from his sister and another of Mary's illegitimate half-brothers, John Stewart. In the perpetual see-saw of Scottish politics, this Bothwell had become identified with Ultra-Protestant hatred for the Catholic earls, and also aristocratic dislike of the new policies which James's servant, John Maitland of Thirlestane, was attempting to introduce. Maitland's name also had a Marian echo: he was brother to Mary's servant, Maitland of Lethington. He had become a member of the Privy Council in 1583 and Secretary of State to the King in 1584. James was fortunate to enjoy the counsels and assiduous work of this wise and subtle negotiator, who for the next ten

OPPOSITE Anne of Denmark; portrait by Marcus Gheeraerts the Younger, *c.* 1605–10.

Newes from Scotland.

James became obsessed by witches in the middle years of his reign in Scotland, his fears aroused by the trials of the North Berwick witches in 1590–1.

ABOVE A woodcut from *Newes from Scotland* shows the Devil preaching to the witches of North Berwick. The storm they supposedly raised against the King's ships returning from Norway is shown in the top left corner.

RIGHT James interrogating Agnes Sampson and three of her fellow witches. He claimed that she told him details of his conversation on his wedding night with Anne of Denmark.

56

years would contribute much to the consolidation of his position in Scotland. However, it was hardly to be expected that a policy which has been described as 'general pacification, economy and efficiency' would appeal to the aristocracy as a whole. Discord was therefore as much present as ever in Scotland.

The introduction of the subject of Scottish witchcraft into the texture of these political disputes was coincidental rather than inevitable. Although much ink has been spilt on the subject of James's apparent lifelong obsession with witchcraft and demonology, the latest research by Christina Larner has stressed how comparatively uninterested he was in such matters before the witchcraft trials. In his early manhood he never displayed that pathological hatred of witches which he demonstrated in the last years of his Scottish rule. Once he reached England and safety his emotional interest in the subject died away. For all Shakespeare's tribute to the cult in the shape of *Macbeth,* there is no evidence, for example, that James even knew of the Lancashire witch trials, let alone tried to attend them. He remained intellectually interested in the subject, but that was characteristic of him. The problem of when was a witch not a witch could be calculated to entrance his attention. It was while pestering Sir John Harington along these lines as to why he thought Satan concentrated on 'ancient women', that James received the witty reply – did not the Scriptures teach them that 'the devil walketh in dry places'?

But there was a middle period, critical years in which James shivered in his royal shoes at the mention of witches, and finally wrote his own tract on the subject, the *Demonologie* of 1597. This was primarily because the North Berwick witchcraft trials introduced the fatal element of the King's person, and his personal safety, into their proceedings. It is suggested by Christina Larner that James had acquired his interest in witchcraft and the idea of the Demonic Pact during his winter's stay with his bride at the Danish Court. It was therefore an unfortunate coincidence that the North Berwick trials seem to provide crucial evidence that the Demonic Pact was being used treasonably to overthrow the King. It was a terrible thing if demonology were to become mixed with practical politics. James's interest in the trials led him to send for one or two of the witches, and be fearfully impressed by what he heard: one, Agnes Sampson, was supposed to have repeated to him things he whispered to the Queen on their wedding night, matters which he swore that all the devils in hell could not have discovered.

The introduction of Francis Bothwell's far more dangerous objectives – he was reputed to have ordained the destruction of the King by witchcraft – was likely to arouse all James's latent paranoia about his own safety. It emerged, for example, that the impudent witches had been casting a judicious mixture of cats and joints of dead bodies into the sea, in order to raise storms while the King was on his nuptial journey. With reference to Bothwell, there was talk of wax images and other sinister developments leading to the death of the King, 'that another might rule in his Majesty's place and the government might go to the Devil'. In James's *Demonologie,* it was significant that the capacity of witches to use wax images and raise storms was still emphasised, along with more intellectual arguments concerning the equality or otherwise of the Devil's powers with those of God.

Bothwell was duly imprisoned, but James's terrors for his own safety were scarcely allayed when the Wizard Earl proceeded to escape from his incarceration in Edinburgh Castle. In view of the obvious sympathy of many of the lords towards him, it proved impossible to recapture Bothwell. On the Borders, for example, Lord Home set out to apprehend him, but promptly joined the outlaw 'to his Majesty's greater contempt'. On 27 December 1591, the lawlessness of Scotland and the perils of James received a dramatic demonstration when Bothwell actually bearded the King at Holyrood. With a number of unruly followers, he pursued James to a remote tower, set fire to his door and that of Maitland, and tried to break them both down with hammers. The King was finally saved by a gathering from Edinburgh town. But one has only to try to imagine – if possible – similar treatment being accorded to Elizabeth and Cecil in England, where Essex committed a major crime for merely interrupting the Queen at her toilette, to understand the vast difference in the circumstances of the two sovereigns and the two countries.

In January 1592, a proclamation was made against Bothwell,

58

PALATIVM REGIVM EDINENSE,
quod & Cænobium S. Crucis.
The royal palace of holy rood-hous. by I.G.

thought to be penned by the King himself, offering a reward to any who would kill him. The offer was not taken up. On the contrary, Bothwell remained triumphantly at large, now terrorising the King by his proximity, now retreating, but ever menacing him by the possibilities of sudden, violent, lethal intrusion. His behaviour would have tried the peace of mind of a far more stable and courageous personality than James. In addition, it must be remembered that James was without a standing army of any sort, without even a proper force of followers, and could be fairly said, as Bothwell's conduct proved, to be at the mercy of any rebellious noble who was the fortunate possessor of the loyal band that James lacked.

It was typical of the times that when letters of fire and sword were given to the Earl of Huntly to prosecute against the Earl of Bothwell, Huntly chose to use them to kill his own enemy, the Earl of Moray, in a particularly despicable crime. The

An engraving of the palace of Holyrood in the sixteenth century.

contemporary ballad of lamentation at the cruel carnage of the 'Bonnie Earl' sums up much of the local despair that such things could and did happen unchecked:

> Ye Highlands and Ye Lowlands
> O where hae ye been?
> They hae slain the Earl of Moray
> And hae laid him on the green.

The scandalous incident was given a further unpleasant twist by the suggestion – for which there is no foundation – that the Bonnie Earl had been the Queen's lover. Maitland's innocence is more open to question, and he may have participated secretly in the murder plot. King James, in a nasty interview with the incensed Presbyterian ministers, was left protesting that he had as little to do with Moray's death as David in the Bible with the slaughter of Abner by Joab.

Was James now to levy war against Huntly – the leading Catholic in the kingdom – as the ministers not surprisingly suggested? But James was becoming adroit at avoiding such confrontations. He had after all skated with difficulty but with success through the delicate period surrounding the failure of the Spanish Armada; in opposition to the powerful Huntly in the north and Lord Maxwell in the west (another Catholic) he had taken a stand against Spain and had actually compelled Maxwell's submission. It was the same notion of divided favours, which had led James, at the age of twenty-one, to cause the bitterest enemies of the state to walk hand in hand through the streets in Edinburgh. It was now the occasion to lean the other way and try to conciliate the Catholic lords, who, however badly Huntly might have behaved, still remained James's best possible bastion against the Presbyterian ministers. If utterly repudiated, they were also capable of raising their intrigues with the foreign Catholic powers to dangerous levels. From James's point of view, it was prudent to involve himself also in secret negotiations with these Catholic powers – so long as Elizabeth's subsidy, which decreased when the rumours of James's Catholic intrigues grew too strong, was not cancelled.

In the meantime, in the sphere of religion, the Black Acts, which had re-established the ecclesiastic authority of the King in 1584, had not maintained their full force for long. In August

John Maitland of Thirlestane, Lord Chancellor of Scotland; miniature by an unknown artist c. 1590.

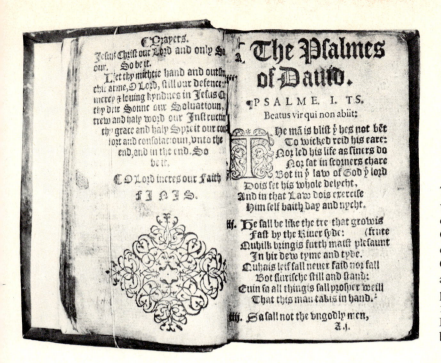

This Psalm Book, found with a short Prayer Book or Book of Common Order, is the only known copy in Scots printed in Gothic type. The psalms are the metrical version, published in Edinburgh in 1564, and derived from English and Genevan books of 1562.

1590, James had delivered a speech in the General Assembly in which he appeared to revoke his previous views and support the Scottish Presbyterian Church once more. In the Parliament of 1592, he consented to a new Act by which the full Presbyterian system was once more restored, and the bishops once again banished from the polity. Such a reverse, however, was more a sign of James's feel for balances than his waning control: the royal position was not affected by the new state of affairs, and it has been suggested that Maitland, in particular, saw in the absence of the bishops an opportunity for the Crown's authority to flourish without intermediate interference. Certainly, the new Act seduced the ministers away from their prolonged political opposition to James, which in itself was a notable improvement. It was satisfying that this same Parliament passed a sentence of forfeiture on the errant Earl of Bothwell. With his Catholic earls to protect him against Bothwell, his ministers to support him against the Catholics, his feelers towards foreign Catholic conspiracy, his Protestant money from Elizabeth, his Maitland to assist and inspire these paradoxical policies, in 1592 James was reaching out towards the one principle by which Scotland might be governed successfully – juggle and rule.

3
The Middle Way

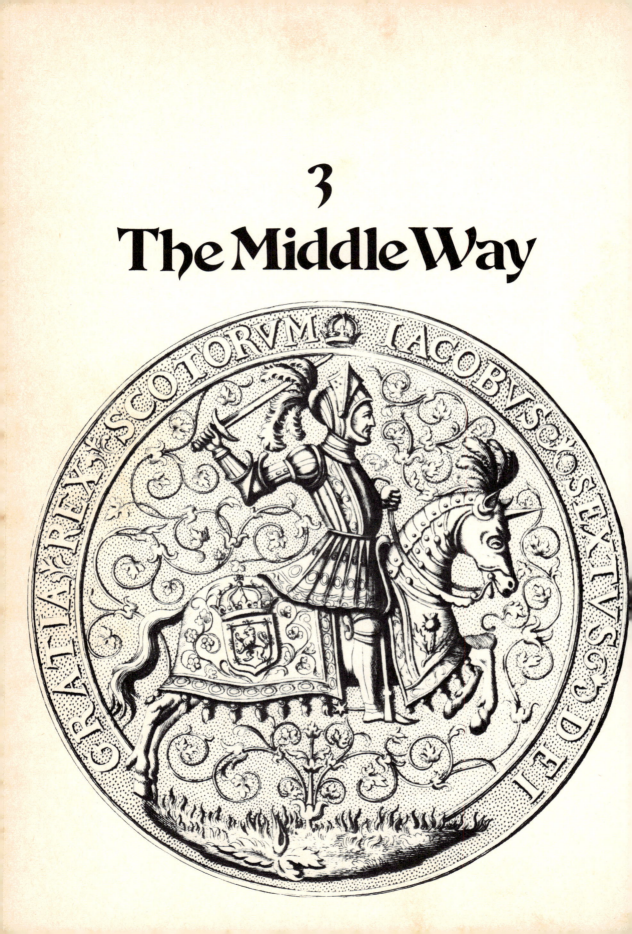

I am ever for the medium in everything.
Between foolish rashness and extreme length,
there is a middle way.

King James

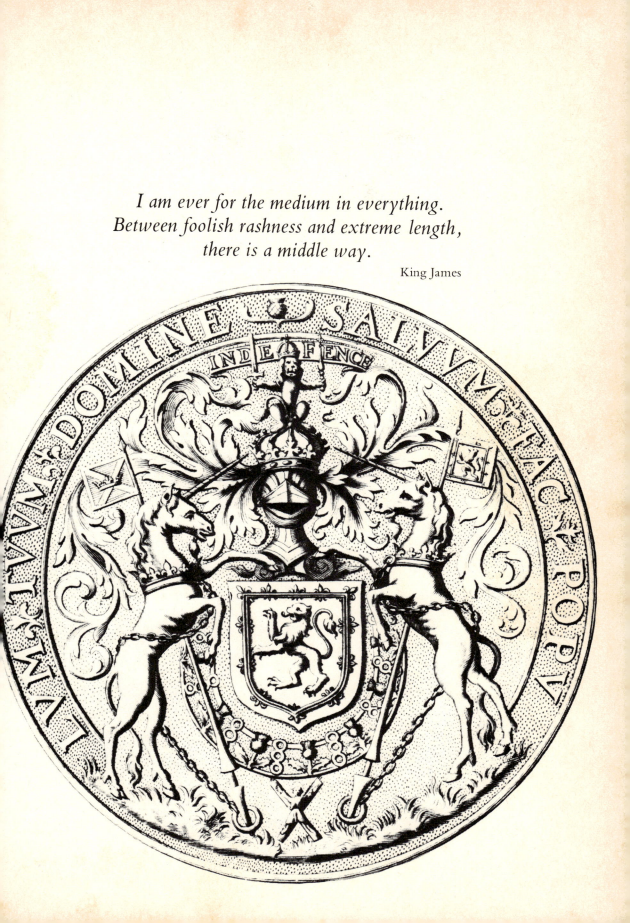

IT TURNED OUT that the early 1590s had marked the climax of James's struggles with his aristocracy. Nevertheless their death-throes were still violent: James can be pardoned for exclaiming at one point that he lamented his estate and accounted 'his fortune to be worse than any prince living'. Hardly had the Parliament of 1592 attempted to soothe down the ferment attendant on Moray's death, than Bothwell renewed his maniacal attacks on the King's person. This time he arrived at Falkland – James's own palace in Fife – with three hundred men, with the avowed intention of beating down the gate with a battering ram. It was not until morning that he ceased besieging the tower where poor King James had been incarcerated for his own safety. A year later, rushing from his bedchamber at Holyrood at a sudden commotion, the King found his evil genius Bothwell, kneeling with drawn sword. The Wizard Earl had seized the royal palace. Shouting 'Treason' James rattled the door to the Queen's chamber but found it bolted; he then turned on his persecutor with the courage of despair, saying that he was a sovereign King, twenty-seven years of age, and he would prefer death to shame and captivity. 'Strike,' replied Bothwell dramatically in response, tending his own sword.

But Bothwell had at last, it seemed, gone too far. An agreement was made by which he would finally stand trial for the old witchcraft charge still hanging over him. Although it was understood that he would be acquitted, he was then expected to retire from Court. And Bothwell's power as a political leader had indubitably waned. There was a final raid in April 1594 when James was obliged to retreat rapidly from the menace of Bothwell's horsemen, back to the security of Edinburgh. But in April 1595, after the failure of his final conspiracy, Bothwell left Scotland for ever.

Similarly with the Catholic earls, James underwent some final traumatic encounters before achieving the sort of solution which freed him from future cares in their direction. Later in 1592, James was accused of being involved in a Catholic conspiracy. It was therefore particularly prudent to embark on a campaign against the Catholic magnates of the north to call attention to his lack of Catholic sympathies. Unfortunately he failed to capture his enemies in the north, and subsequently failed to persuade Parliament to declare them forfeit. Their next insurgency involved an alliance with Bothwell in the south to balance their activities in the north. But the Spanish assistance for which they had hoped did not materialise. The Catholic earls were gradually brought to the position where their best course appeared to lie in temporary departure from the shores of Scotland. When Huntly returned in 1597 it was actually as a pseudo-Protestant, promising repentance and emendation of his ways to the General Assembly of the Kirk.

The truth was that not only James but Scotland as a whole was becoming wearied of the unsullied rebelliousness of their aristocracy. The way was becoming clear for the formation of a type of middle party, including men of such diverse opinions as the Treasurer, Glamis, Lord John Hamilton, and the Catholic Homes. A *via media* had always represented the best hope of a Scottish king. And now with the most cruelly ebullient of James's challengers fled, there seemed a good chance of pursuing it successfully. As he said of himself when in England, he was ever for the medium in everything. 'Between foolish rashness and extreme length, there is a middle way.' In the remaining years of James's Scottish rule, he would draw increasing support from the rising middle classes. It was a policy which his Chancellor Maitland had believed in strongly, although Maitland had undergone too many passages of arms in the course of his office to survive the rows of 1592. He was obliged to retire from public service and died a few years later. Nevertheless in the use of the lairds, the burgesses of the towns, and the recognition that in these men lay another force in Scotland other than that of the nobility, the fruitful hand of Maitland may be discerned. James appointed no more supreme officials, saying in his joking way that 'he would no more use chancellors or other great men in those his causes, but such as he might convict and were hangable'. But with the cooperative nobles rewarded by temporal lordships, erected on lands previously held by the Catholic Church, and the uncooperative ones departed, he had no great need of such.

There had always been a theoretical right of the Stuarts to rule, even though their powers had been practically limited to a vast extent by the pretensions of the aristocracy. Now James came to enjoy that right in a manner far less trammelled than

previously in the history of the dynasty. It was significant that in February 1594, at the birth of James's heir Prince Henry, the people went 'daft for mirth'. For it is not only kings on whom perpetual civil confusion palls; the people also pine for security. James's developed tenacity of character, his crab-like quality of hanging on in an impossible situation, had finally snatched a kind of victory out of what had seemed an almost certain defeat.

In the more stable conditions which now prevailed, a fair period of economic growth was enjoyed in Scotland. It was not in general marked by much industrial development, with the exception of coal, but the material prosperity of the people increased. Not that James's own finances ever improved much: on the contrary, they continued so deplorable that in October 1596 a committee of eight, known for that reason as the

66

View of Edinburgh in the sixteenth century. The waters of Leith can be seen in the foreground of the picture, the castle on the left.

Octavians, was set up to improve his revenues. Eighteen months of heroic effort saw little advance, however, and in any case the clergy were annoyed with the innovation, particularly as some of the Octavians were suspected of papist leanings. The Octavians vanished. James's own situation remained so parlous that in 1599 his Comptroller absconded rather than face the responsibilities of it. His difficulties were only enhanced by the rudimentary system of taxation and highly inefficient Exchequer methods of accounting. Yet James, for all his acute poverty, was merely the poor King of a poor country, and one in which it was still possible to live via goods and chattels, rather than money. In this, as in so many ways, Scotland was in marked contrast to England.

Parallel with the improvement in James's effective status as King, came his development of his theoretical position. Between the Kirk's view of the King's rights, and those which James now expounded, there were obviously irreconcilable differences. While the Presbyterians attacked the King's pretensions to head the Church, on the grounds that the civil magistrate must be beneath the ecclesiastical power, James put forward exactly the opposite view that the sovereign had an individual right, derived directly from God, to his throne. James's *Trew Law of Free Monarchies,* originally printed anonymously in 1598, also stressed the hereditary nature of his rights – and it was not a complete coincidence that James's claim to the English throne was based on hereditary not legal right. But his propositions concerning the divine origins of a King's authority were far-reaching indeed. Even a bad King, he argued, had his inalienable rights over the people, on the grounds that he had been sent by God to punish the people – a doctrine which was about as far from the famous tenets of tyrant-removal once preached by his tutor Buchanan as could be imagined. As James Welwood was to point out in his *Memoirs,* divine right permeated James's writings while he was still in Scotland, because 'he had been kept short of it in his Native Country'. James had endured a great deal of aristocratic insurrection, and was still obliged to suffer under the denunciations of the Kirk and the ministers. When he wrote that since Kings existed before Parliaments, they were thus the makers of laws, and not the laws the makers of Kings, or that the King was an absolute

thairfore my sonne to thir puritanis uerrie pestis in the kirk & commonwell
of Skotland, quhom be long experience I haue founde na desairtis can
oblishe, oathis nor promeisis binde brauling nathing bot Sedicion &
calumnies aspyring without measure rayling without reason & making
thaire awin imaginacions without any warrande of the worde the Squaire
of thaire conscience, I protest before the greate god & sen James
he we upon my testament it is na place for me to lee in) that I neuer founde
with any heelande or bordoure of thefis sa great ingratitude & sa
manie lees & uyle periuries as I haue founde with sum of thaime &
suffer not the pryncypallis of thame to brooke youre lands gif ye lyke to sitt
at rest except ye halde keip thame for trying youre pacience as Socrates
did ane euill wyfe & for preseruation againis thaire poison incresence &
aduaunce quhom of god be praised thair is nou a reasonable nomber
and the godlie learned & modest men of the ministerie be thaire preferrement
to bishopprik & benefices ye shall not onlie banishe thaire parritie quhilke
can not agree with a monarchie but ye also sall reestablishe the aulde institucion of
thre estates in parliament quhilke can na other weyes be done but in this I hoap
gif god spaire me dayes to make you a faire entres, alwayes quhaire I leaue follow
ye my foote steppis & the first that raillis againis you punishe with the rigoure
of the law for I haue in my dayes ouer hurstin thame with ouer mekill reason &
to end my aduyce anent the kirk estait cherishe na mair then a gude pastoure
hate na mair then a proude puritane thinking it ane of youre fairest styles
to be called a louing noorishe father to the kirk seeing all the kirkis within youre
dominions planted with goode pastoures the doctrine & discipline maintened in

creation, without any particular reciprocal duties, James was as much arguing against counter theories headily preached in Scotland as he was propounding his own. Although, therefore, the *Trew Law* could have been read in advance, like Hitler's *Mein Kampf,* as a guide to James's future intentions, the true genesis of the work lay in his Scottish past, and not in his British future.

Basilikon Doron, written for the enlightenment of his son Henry and printed in 1598, contained some startling if magnificent claims: it also had that prerequisite of all best-sellers, timing: it happened to be on sale in England within a few days of Elizabeth's death, and was thus seized avidly and bought profusely. The dedicatory sonnet is a bold confession of faith: Kings have received from God himself 'the style of Gods' in order to wield his own sceptre on their respective thrones. Again and again in the text James refers to a sovereign as 'a little God'. Kings are 'the breathing images of God', 'God Lieutenants', and finally 'even by God himself they are called Gods'. But there is an obvious difference between these hyperbolic claims, extended in Scotland against the equally radical claims of the Scottish Kirk, and a blueprint for how James intended to try to rule England. King James, in these writings which were to be so much quoted later, was in the position of a child writing a hopeful sketch for how the grown-up world could be better run.

In Scotland it was symptomatic of James's cautious advances that he now emerged triumphant from further encounters with two of his ancient bugbears, the Kirk and the Ultra-Protestant nobles. Contests there still were, but the King no longer wandered lonely and hunted across his own kingdom as he had in the demon-haunted days of the Wizard Earl of Bothwell. When the Kirk decided to voice their criticisms of the Octavians, it was Andrew Melville who headed the (uninvited) deputation. This time it was Melville who overreached himself: he described James to his face as 'God's silly vassal'. 'And, sir,' said Melville, 'when you were in your swaddling clothes, Christ Jesus reigned freely in this land in spite of all his enemies.' He had overestimated the affronts it was still possible to give to the royal dignity: for not only did James manage to secure from the Kirk the hypocritical submission of the Catholic Huntly

OPPOSITE A page from the manuscript of James's *Basilikon Doron* published in 1598. The book sets out his views on kingship and the duties of the sovereign for the instruction of his son, Prince Henry.

mentioned above, but the General Assembly of 1597 showed how far James had summed up the Scottish rules of success: by having it summoned at Perth, in the Highlands, he ensured that the shadow of the local territorial magnates, the Catholic earls, would loom over the neighbourhood clergy. As for the rest, they would not find it particularly easy to reach Perth, not only on grounds of distance but also because they were responsible for their own travelling expenses. Melville and his group denounced the Perth gathering as being no true Assembly, but James received from it nonetheless some welcome reassurances concerning the royal authority. Melville's theory of the two kingdoms, with that of the Church being superior to that of the State, was not upheld.

In August 1600, that mysterious incident known as the Gowrie Conspiracy involved one way and another many of the old warring elements of the kingdom. The aristocratic family from which it took its name, the Ruthvens, headed by the Earl of Gowrie, were among the chiefs of the Ultra-Protestant Scots, and had incidentally in June strongly opposed James's financial demands in Parliament. As a historical conundrum, the Gowrie Conspiracy is the second of the four affecting the life of King James, of which the death of his father at Kirk o' Field was the first, and the Gunpowder Plot and the Overbury Murder were to be the third and fourth. It is however the only one of the four in which he was intimately concerned, which is why it will be examined at greater length. Like James's attitude to witches subsequent to the North Berwick trials, one feels instinctively that his behaviour to the Ruthvens on this occasion fits best into the general pattern of his troubles with the nobility. But it must be admitted that this is one of those peculiarly baffling mysteries where no one solution fits all the facts.

Those facts of the case not in dispute are, briefly, as follows: on 5 August, King James, who was out hunting near his own palace of Falkland, broke off the expedition unexpectedly after a visit from the Earl of Gowrie's younger brother, the personable twenty-year-old Master of Ruthven. He rode to Gowrie House at Perth, and was there entertained under the auspices of Greysteil, Earl of Gowrie himself. An improvised dinner took place, because Gowrie was apparently not aware of the honour

in store. After dinner, the King retired with the young Master. His own servants were not apprised of this development and when they asked where the King had gone, were told by Gowrie that he had left. Fortunately they did not totally accept this surprising explanation, since some time later the King's voice was heard shouting 'Treason, treason' out of a turret window. The room in which he was found proved to be bolted from the inside. However the ensuing rescue attempt by James's attendants turned out successfully ; and both the Master and the Earl were killed in the process.

Such a bizarre incident raises a number of questions. First, what on earth was in King James's mind to make this sudden foray towards Gowrie House, into the heartland of that family from whom, quite apart from recent incidents of opposition, he had traditionally much to fear ? The present Gowrie's father had been executed for treason in 1584; the Raid of Ruthven had constituted one of the most poignant of James's youthful humiliations, and going further back beyond his own memory, but not beyond that of vividly recounted legend – it was an Earl of Gowrie who had held the steel at his mother's pregnant belly during the slaughter of Riccio. In view of the fact that James now pursued the remaining members of the Ruthven family with

An engraving of Falkland Palace in the seventeenth century by John Slezer. It was while hunting near Falkland that James set off for Gowrie House.

71

ruthless vengeance, to the distress of Queen Anne who numbered Lady Beatrice Ruthven among her favourite attendants,
some convincing explanation was necessary.

James's official description of how all these amazing events had
come to pass was certainly vivid. The Master of Ruthven, he
said, had lured him to Gowrie House with a strange story of a
pot of gold, which James was supposed to investigate. Once
dinner was over, the Master, who had shown all day a 'smiling
countenance', led the King away, ostensibly to see the famous
gold, but introduced him instead into a little study where there
was a fellow armed with a dagger. The Master locked the door
and then 'changing his Countenance, putting his Hat on his
Head and drawing the Dagger ... held the point to the King's
breast, avowing now that the King behoved to be in his Will
and used as he List', Gowrie would come and talk with him.
Since James was armed only with his hunting horn, 'which
he had not gotten Leisure to lay from him', there was little he
could do in this predicament except yell for help. In fact he was
only rescued in the nick of time because the Gowrie porter con-
fessed the truth of the King's whereabouts to his servants. It was

72

no wonder that James's first action on being liberated, according to his own account, was to sink to his knees in gratitude to God for his deliverance. It does indeed sound positively miraculous.

Naturally the defeated and debased Ruthvens put forward their own story. According to this, it was King James who had in some manner inveigled the young Master to Falkland, in order to pretend that his own arrival in Perth was at the Master's instigation. James's object was the ultimate destruction of the Ruthvens. The best piece of circumstantial evidence on the Ruthvens' side is the lack of preparations at Gowrie House for the King's arrival (against which one should put Gowrie's untrue assurance to the royal servants that the King had left). But there is a basic improbability, surely, in any story which depends on the timid James using his own person as a decoy in a trap of his own making. If he wished to destroy the Ruthvens, there were many better ways of doing it than plunging into their own territory in such an insecure manner. Still less would he have endured being locked into a small room with a healthy and vigorous young man like the Master – a situation in which he might well have perished before his servants reached him.

Was there then some other explanation which scandal prevented either the King or the Ruthvens from making fully known? The theory that Queen Anne had the Master as her lover may be dismissed, but perhaps James had some homosexual imbroglio with the Master? If so, it still leaves the surprising break-off from the Falkland hunt to Gowrie House unexplained. Alternatively, politics being generally a stronger motive than sex, there may have been some involvement of the Gowries in affairs outside Scotland which would explain these peculiar events if we could ever unravel them. This has been conjectured most recently by George Malcolm Thomson: since this was the period of the Essex conspiracy, James may have suspected Gowrie of being tempted into some political action, and even Cecil may have played some part in it all. The ensuing fracas at Gowrie House resulted when Gowrie declined to come to Falkland at James's invitation but sent his brother; so James was obliged to return to Perth, but being prepared to strike, where Gowrie was not, emerged the victor.

On balance however the King's version, or the kernel of it, is to be preferred, as Andrew Lang argued. James himself spoke

the truest word about his own character, and the unlikelihood
that he of all people would initiate such a rash and complicated
conspiracy. He told an Edinburgh minister who refused to
believe his explanation : 'It is known very well that I was never
blood-thirsty. If I would have taken their lives, I had causes
enough ; I needed not to hazard myself so.' If one accepts, for
these reasons of personality, or put more crudely sheer cowardice, that James did not weave a plot, it follows that some sort
of plot must have been set up by the Gowries. Precisely what,
will never be known.

Perhaps the pot of gold was actually a true story as David
Mathew has tentatively suggested – James did need money
and there were debts between James and the Ruthvens. Perhaps it was the familiar Scottish case of a disguised kidnapping,
from which the Ruthvens hoped to squeeze further concessions along the lines of political Protestantism from the
incarcerated King. Whatever their intentions, the plot went
awry, either through the King's terror or an unplanned
quarrel ; where no deaths were intended, either those of James
or the Ruthvens, it was the latter who ended up dead on the
floor. It was significant that afterwards, when the King asked
the ministers, in addition to thanking God publicly for his
deliverance, also to describe exactly what had happened
according to his own official version, five of them refused.
While they 'gladly agreed' to express their gratitude for his
escape, 'to declare and preach the manner in particular as a
truth of God out of the pulpit' they said politely, was impossible
'because the informations were divers and uncertain'. Of these
five, the most obdurate, Robert Bruce, was driven out to
England. For all the King's annoyance, the ministers' words
were probably the best comment on the Gowrie Conspiracy.

Yet James had emerged from the whole obscure business not
only alive but also triumphant. The forfeiture and dispersal of
the Ruthven family was one advantage. In November 1600,
James secured another advantage in his perpetual battle with
the clerical zealots of the Kirk. In an Assembly held in July,
James had suggested that bishops should be nominated as
representatives of the Church in Parliament. This tentative
move in favour of political Episcopalianism he had failed to
bring off. Now, although his ding-dong battle with the extreme

74

clergy continued to the end of his Scottish rule and beyond, he was sufficiently in control to nominate three bishops himself. This trio were given seats in the Scottish Parliament. It was the thin end of the Episcopalian wedge.

During these last years, James governed Scotland most adequately through his Council. He laboured for peace, and secured it in some measure, even in that notoriously untranquil area of the Highlands. He displayed good intentions, at least towards the Western Isles, seen in an Act of 1597 for planting three burghs of Kintyre, Lochaber and on the Isle of Lewis, and the abortive venture of the Stornoway plantations. As a result, an Englishman reported that the poor people there prayed for him and his labours. The Borders, which were even more lawless if less wild than the Highlands, received their own measure of pacification. It has been pointed out that the celebrated affair of Kinmont Willie, rescued from a prison in English Carlisle by a Scott of Buccleuch, received its fame from the fact that the incident was by now more of an exception than the rule. As for the nobility, although James could not touch their feudal jurisdictions, he did have success in curbing the limits of their private retinues, and thus curtail the possibilities of private wars.

The assumption is that James, who was already making a good King of Scotland, might have made a great King had not the basilisk of the English Crown lured him away from his area of achievement. Even so, on his foundations, Scotland was to enjoy what has been described by one distinguished Scottish historian as 'forty years of unprecedented tranquillity' – from the riot in Edinburgh on 17 December 1596 to another riot in Edinburgh on 23 July 1637. It is idle to blame him for his attraction to England any more than one would blame George I for deserting Hanover in 1714. That was what kingship was about. But in terms of the future, it is interesting to speculate what might have happened not only to James but to Scotland, if Elizabeth had actually produced an heir. Leaving aside the man's ambitions, the country might have been happier in the long run. As it was, the English basilisk was by now smiling.

Time had not stood still in England. By 1600 Elizabeth could no longer hold age at bay. Although James assured her flatteringly in his correspondence that she would last as long as

OPPOSITE Fiddler, bagpiper and other figures on carved oak panels, probably from Threave Castle, Kirkcudbrightshire, about 1600.

the sun and moon, that prospect seemed increasingly unlikely. The question of the next ruler of England would, one way or the other, soon have to be solved. James's own position had by this time acquired a new stability from those chancy intriguing days of the early 1590s when he had at least contemplated some kind of foreign invasion with Catholic and Spanish aid to secure his rights. Exactly what did these rights consist of? It must be realised that James never had the incontrovertible claim to the English throne which might be suggested, reading history backwards, by the ease of eventual accession.

It was true that James was the senior descendant of King Henry VII of England, as his mother had been before him. The elder of Henry VII's two daughters, Margaret Tudor, had married King James IV of Scotland as her first husband, and from this union James descended directly. After the line of Henry VII's only son, Henry VIII, died out with his remaining living child Elizabeth, James would have the best purely hereditary claim. But the situation was not quite so simple. According to the will of Henry VIII, all aliens were to be excluded from the succession. James, born in Scotland, was held to be an alien, particularly as his attempts to recover the English Lennox estates of his (English) father had failed. In this respect, James's own first cousin Arbella Stuart, only child of Darnley's brother Charles, might be considered to have a better claim because she was actually English. On the other hand her claim still came through Margaret Tudor via her second marriage to another Scot. Although Arbella was never a horse to be ignored altogether in the race, it was also held against her that her Protestant religious views were thought to waver; at one point the Pope even supported her pretensions.

Then there were the various descendants of Henry VII's second daughter, Mary Tudor (to whom the will of Henry VIII had given specific precedence over the descendants of Margaret). Here the problem was not one of alien birth, but of the validity of marriages and legitimacy of children. Mary's own marriage had been doubtful, that of her grand-daughter, Lady Catherine Grey, even more so. The Grey girls, who were much disliked by Queen Elizabeth, had an unfortunate propensity for misalliances, and the youngest of them was also virtually mentally deficient. Of Mary Tudor's descendants,

OPPOSITE Elizabeth I with Time and Death; an allegorical portrait painted after her death by an unknown artist.

OPPOSITE Esmé Stuart
Sieur d'Aubigny, James's
cousin and his first
favourite, created
Duke of Lennox in 1580.

the best hope was probably the Earl of Derby, now married to Cecil's niece, if her own marriage had been valid. Looking to England's more remote royal past, there was the Earl of Huntingdon, who descended from the Duke of Clarence, the brother of Edward IV. And, surprising as it might seem, there was a Spanish claimant, in the shape of the Infanta Clara Eugenia, daughter of the King of Spain.

The Infanta's claims were traced through descent from John of Gaunt, quite apart from the fact that Mary Queen of Scots was erroneously supposed to have willed England away from Protestant James to Philip II at the last moment. The claims of the Infanta, ably argued by that formidable Jesuit apologist Father Robert Parsons, were probably never seriously considered by Robert Cecil, despite rumours to the contrary. In the same way James in the end prudently decided against an invasion from the north, on the excellent grounds that if his title were recognised, 'we have attained our design without stroke of sword'. But it was not until late on in the decade that the future master and man, King James and Cecil, came to recognise that each represented the other's best interest in the future.

In August 1596 James acknowledged his hopes towards Elizabeth by the placatory gesture of naming his eldest daughter after her. Once again the Queen was godmother, but how different were the circumstances from those of James's own baptism thirty years before! Elizabeth was the sole sponsor, 'the whole Honour in the Solemnity and of all the Ceremonies, was given alone to Her Majesty, with good observance of all due Compliments' – there was now no King of France or Duke of Savoy to share the honours. Queen Elizabeth omitted to send a present – no more gold fonts were forthcoming although James wore new socks for this occasion, of crimson velvet laced with gold. But the baby was given the name of the Queen by the English ambassador, after which she was 'cried and called by the Lyon Herald, Lady Elizabeth, first daughter of Scotland'. It will be remembered how Elizabeth's proxy at James's own Catholic baptism had skulked at the chapel door.

For all this flattering public demonstration of cousinly obeisance, as late as 1599 (although he denied it afterwards), James probably signed a propitiatory letter to the Pope beginning *Beatissime Pater*; of this Elizabeth would certainly not have

80

The English Succession

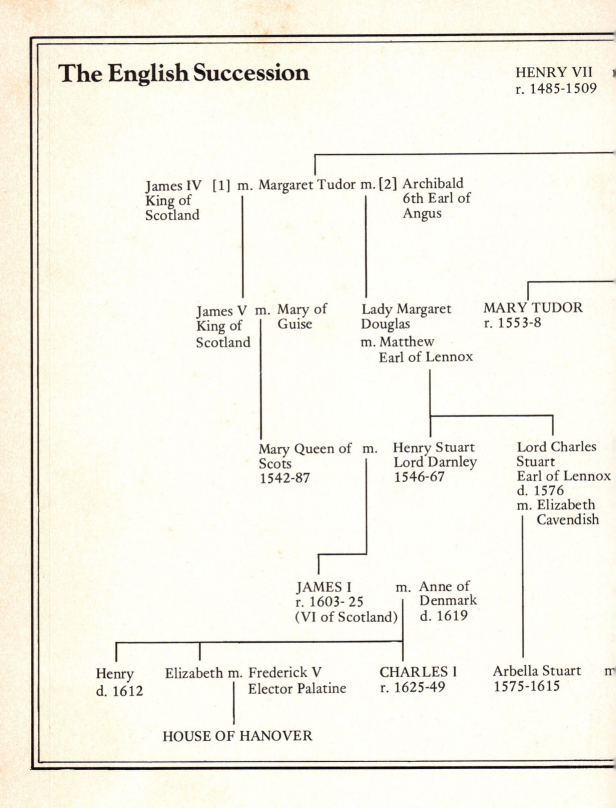

James IV [1] m. Margaret Tudor m. [2] Archibald
King of   6th Earl of
Scotland   Angus

James V m. Mary of   Lady Margaret   MARY TUDOR
King of   Guise   Douglas   r. 1553-8
Scotland   m. Matthew
                              Earl of Lennox

Mary Queen of m.   Henry Stuart   Lord Charles
Scots   Lord Darnley   Stuart
1542-87   1546-67   Earl of Lennox
                                         d. 1576
                                         m. Elizabeth
                                           Cavendish

JAMES I   m. Anne of
r. 1603- 25   Denmark
(VI of Scotland) d. 1619

Henry   Elizabeth m. Frederick V   CHARLES I   Arbella Stuart   m
d. 1612   Elector Palatine   r. 1625-49   1575-1615

HOUSE OF HANOVER

Elizabeth of York

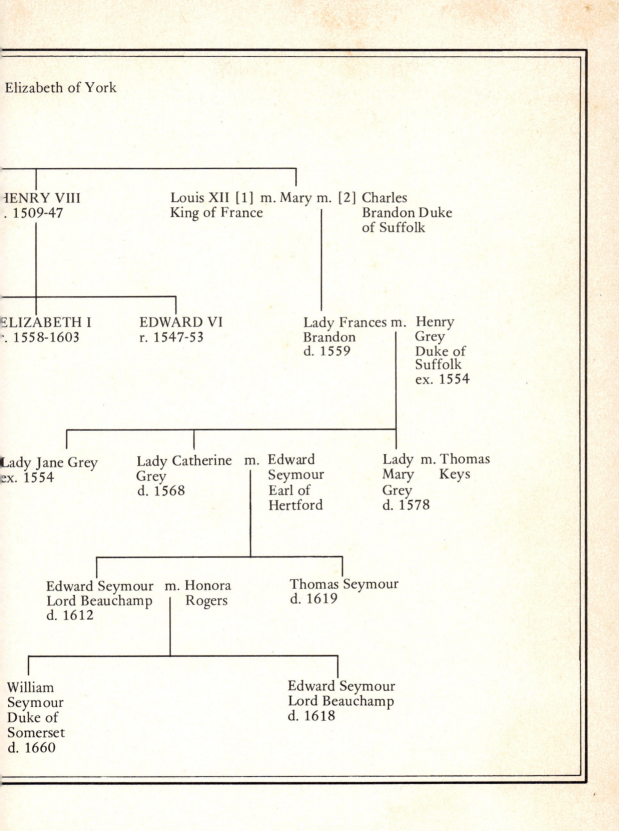

HENRY VIII
. 1509-47

Louis XII [1] m. Mary m. [2] Charles
King of France   Brandon Duke
of Suffolk

ELIZABETH I
. 1558-1603

EDWARD VI
r. 1547-53

Lady Frances m. Henry
Brandon   Grey
d. 1559   Duke of
Suffolk
ex. 1554

Lady Jane Grey
ex. 1554

Lady Catherine m. Edward
Grey   Seymour
d. 1568   Earl of
Hertford

Lady m. Thomas
Mary   Keys
Grey
d. 1578

Edward Seymour m. Honora
Lord Beauchamp   Rogers
d. 1612

Thomas Seymour
d. 1619

William
Seymour
Duke of
Somerset
d. 1660

Edward Seymour
Lord Beauchamp
d. 1618

A map of Scotland from John Speed's *Theatre of Great Britain*, 1610. The borders are decorated with portraits of James and his family.

approved. James also continued to woo the English Catholics with promises, and even corresponded with the Earl of Tyrone in Ireland. Such devious policies bore fruits : the Pope began to acquiesce in the possibility of James's title ; but they also smacked of treachery to Elizabeth if discovered. Most dangerous of all, from the point of view of losing all he had gained, was James's involvement in the many fringe ramifications of the Essex conspiracy.

Essex, in a manner typical of his rash and impatient nature, suffered under the totally false belief that Elizabeth, because she was getting old, 'could be brought to nothing but by a kind of necessity and authority'. He achieved a certain success in spreading the *canard* that Cecil was favouring the Infanta, but otherwise his imprudent attempts to force the Queen's hand, including his unsolicited return from his command in Ireland, met with a tragic if inevitable end. However, it seems likely that James, torn as ever between hope and fear, did allow himself to be at least tainted with intrigue. Essex was apparently in correspondence with James from 1598 on, and there was mention of a 'project' by which James would prepare an army, march to the Borders, and there demand that his royal rights to succeed should be recognised. Irish invaders, under Mountjoy, would join in. James was said to have 'liked the course well, and would prepare himself for it'. An emissary, in the shape of a bookseller called Norton, came to James at Christmas 1600, and asked James to respond with his own emissary. In time James despatched the Earl of Mar, but showing his growing penchant for deliberate delay, was fortunately saved by it – before Mar actually arrived in London, Essex had been executed.

It was not a total coincidence that this piece of indecision had turned out so favourably for the King. James never quite lost his head in the matter of the succession, as Essex, in more senses than one, lost his. He remained aware that while all these factors could gain him the throne, they could also lose it for him. In this he showed a cleverness uncharacteristic of most of the other Stuarts ; at least he understood the art of the possible, and that to wait is often better than to act. In this respect he resembled another product of an unhappy childhood, his cousin Queen Elizabeth, more than his petted mother Mary, or his son Charles I.

It was after Essex's death that Cecil was able to make clear to James two things: firstly, no public recognition could be expected from Elizabeth. She herself had put the subject of succession in a nutshell years back when she observed that the people were ever prone to worship the rising rather than the setting sun. Secondly, James himself was now from the point of view of the majority in England the common-sense candidate, being male, Protestant, possessed of a strong hereditary claim, with children of his own to follow him. Above all, he was already of commensurate rank, and Elizabeth herself was supposed to have observed that none but a King should follow her. Against this background was initiated a curious correspondence in which Cecil secretly trained James in the art of becoming King of England.

The letters themselves (of which Elizabeth knew nothing) were full of the ploys of conspiracy, all much enjoyed by James. Names were given in code. Cecil himself was 10, the Earl of Northumberland 0, James 30, Elizabeth 24 and the Earl of Mar 20. There were dramatic little incidents as when the Queen nearly opened a packet innocently, hearing that it was 'from Scotland', and had to be distracted. The correspondence, which lasted from the spring of 1601 until Elizabeth's death two years later, marked the rise of Cecil's influence over James, as he graduated in the King's letters into the position of James's 'dearest and most truest 10'. He explained his mistress's peculiar mentality to James: as love is blind, so fear is suspicious, 'neither trusteth profession nor heareth reason'. James must reckon with this and avoid untimely interference: then he could sleep safely with regard to his prospects. Cecil recommended steadfastness: let there be found in James 'a heart of adamant in a world of feathers'. Gradually people in England would come to the conclusion that James was Elizabeth's natural successor, as it was put, *in corde* if not *in ore aperto*: in their hearts, if not in open discussion. At the same time James's scanty store of knowledge of the country he wished to inherit was augmented. Moreover he liked what he heard. A process of disenchantment with his native land, born of a lifetime of arduous endeavour, was set in train. He began to think of England as a promised land, or as he expressed it: 'It is a far more barbarous and stiff necked people that I rule over. Saint George surely rides upon a

Robert Devereux,
Earl of Essex, Elizabeth's
last favourite and her
Master of the Horse.
He and his friends lost
power in the struggle with
Robert Cecil; a desperate
rebellion ended in
disaster and his execution.
Portrait by William Segar.

towardly riding horse, where I am daily bursting in daunting a
wild unruly colt.'

And in the fullness of time, the horse of St George did pass
to its eager and optimistic new rider. As Northumberland had
written to James of the ageing Queen 'young bodies may die,
but old ones must out of necessity'. That necessity eventually
came to Elizabeth in March 1603. Her death was preceded by a
phase of great 'dullness and a lethargy', combined with lack of
sleep in the course of which Northumberland told James that

SERO, SED SERIO

people were beginning at last to talk 'freely' of his right. The Queen herself put it more poetically. 'I am not sick,' she said, 'I feel no pain, and yet I pine away.' In his prison cell the Jesuit William Weston noticed the strange silence which descended on the whole city of London in honour of the dying Queen, with no bells and bugles heard, 'as if it were under interdict and divine worship suspended'. In Scotland, James waited at Holyrood. Finally on 24 March a reign which had lasted only nine years longer than James's own, but seemed like a whole era, came to an end. Elizabeth had died 'easily like a ripe apple from a tree' as one diarist put it. At 10.00 a.m. there was a proclamation at Whitehall Gate of James I of England.

What followed, termed by John Chamberlain an 'undignified scramble' northwards, only confirmed how sensible the dead Queen had been to restrict the rays of the rising sun. 'There is much posting that way,' wrote Chamberlain of the frantic trek to Scotland, 'and many run thither of their own errand, as if it were nothing else but first come first served, or that preferment were a goal to be got by footmanship.' If it had been, then the feat of Sir Robert Carey, who had prepared horses posted all along the North road to enable him to be the first to break the news to the new monarch, would certainly have advanced him to high office. As it was, although made Gentleman of the Bedchamber as a reward, he was subsequently denied the post through the hostility of the English Council.

The Council's own official message only reached James five days after Elizabeth's death. But already James had penned a letter to Northumberland, having heard the momentous news, telling him that he wanted to enter England 'as the son and righteous heir of England, with all peace and calmness, and without any kind of alteration in state and government as far as I possibly can'. On 5 April he embarked on what Dr Johnson, a hundred and fifty years later, cynically termed 'the noblest prospect which a Scotchman ever sees … the high road that leads him to England!' King James, without the cynicism, would undoubtedly have agreed.

OPPOSITE Robert Cecil, Earl of Salisbury, who succeeded his father as Elizabeth's chief minister and did much to secure the peaceful accession of James I. He was James's most able and experienced minister during the early years of his reign in England. Portrait by John de Critz, 1602.

4
Of Britain King

…Arthur I am, of Britain King,
Come by good right to claim my seat and throne,
My kingdoms severed to rejoin in one,
To mend what is amiss in everything.

Walter Quin

PREVIOUS PAGES
'The Garden of Plenty';
arch designed by Stephen
Harrison for the entry of
James and Anne to London
in 1604.

OPPOSITE Portrait of
James VI and I attributed to
John de Critz, c. 1605.
In his hat he wears the
jewel of the Mirror of
Great Britain, made in
1604 to symbolise the
union of the kingdoms.
BELOW The Lyte Jewel,
containing a miniature of
James by Hilliard, with a
jewelled cover.

ALTHOUGH THE NEW KING had been proclaimed in the south as James I of England, he himself adopted, without the consent of Parliament, the title of King of Great Britain. It was his own historical obsession, indicating how he intended to present himself to his subjects in the future and remained a phrase considered as peculiarly his : twenty years later a hostile pamphlet would refer angrily to '*your* word, Great Britain'. Both before and after his accession, James laid much emphasis on his British connection. It was true that James was to be, in terms of blood, the most British sovereign to occupy our throne until the present Queen (with the exception of his two childless grand-daughters Mary II and Anne). Nearly half his blood was Scots, as has been seen, and of the remainder, nearly one quarter English. Elizabeth II, from the marriage of her father to Lady Elizabeth Bowes-Lyon, enjoys the same mixture of royal and Scots noble blood. In between the German (Hanoverian and Saxe-Coburg) strain predominated.

That lay ahead. In the meantime a poem published in Edinburgh in 1595 by an Irishman Walter Quin, referring to him as Arthur, 'of Britain King, Come by good right to claim my seat and throne' had much pleased the King. For James took great pleasure in deriving his royal descent from one Brute, king of all the Britons, and as such the founder of a far more ancient pedigree than that of mere Tudors or Stuarts. Throughout his reign, James remained susceptible to those who took part in this genealogical charade. The antiquarian Thomas Lyte, who drew up 'a most royally ennobled genealogy' of James, tactfully starting it at 'Brute, the most noble founder of the Britains', received as a reward the famous Lyte Jewel, which contained a beautiful miniature of the King by Nicholas Hilliard.

So Brute's latest descendant made the long journey south to take up his inheritance. From the poverty and the problems, he was at last, as he said himself, 'like a poor man wandering about forty years in a wilderness and barren soil and now arrived at the land of promise'. And how he enjoyed the opportunities for graciousness which now opened before him, and how many opportunities there proved to be ! As Sir Richard Wilbraham put it, 'It is the manner after the death of a long reigning prince, that by discontented minds or wits starved

for want of employment, many new projects, suits, inventions or infinite complaints are brought to the success instantly.' So knighthoods, three hundred of them, fell in abundance on those who had prudently taken the golden road north to this new Samarkand. James, in his turn, hunting as he went, could not fail to observe the mighty mansions of the English nobility, at Worksop, Doncaster and Belvoir Castle, and wonder at their richness compared to the infinitely smaller Scottish strongholds of his youth : David Mathew has termed them 'vast houses built for splendour and peace', two qualities which had been in short supply in Scotland.

But it must be admitted that the blood of Brute in the veins of King James was less obvious to his new subjects than something rather more recent – and more Scottish. They beheld a middle-aged Scotsman (James was approaching thirty-seven) with a broad Scots accent, a homely fellow, stocky and rather untidy, with a pleasantly convivial manner to his intimates. As an Englishman had remarked, he was the sort of King in Scotland at whose dinner-table all comers had been welcomed in a thoroughly relaxed way. In short, James did not stand on ceremony. That was just the trouble. Not only did he not stand on ceremony, he did not even like it or appreciate its worth. He saw nothing to charm and little to amuse in the spectacle of cheering crowds. That cozening of the common people, which results from a curious adrenalin at contact with the masses, which Elizabeth had possessed to perfection, James neither had nor wished to have. Very soon his indifference to ceremonial became public talk. An Englishman wrote that 'the Accesses of the People made him impatient, that he often dispersed them with Frowns, that we may not say with Curses…'.

His consort Anne was capable of much public sweetness, and accounts of her passage through London, saluting her subjects 'with great mildness' and 'never leaving [off] to bend her body this way and that, that men and women wept for joy', remind one vividly of the stance of the royal family today in similar circumstances. James, however, when told on one occasion that the people wanted to see him, retorted vigorously : 'God's wounds I will pull down my breeches and they shall also see my arse.' Vulgarity apart, the sentiment is one which many figures in the public eye may have shared from time to time, tested by

The coronation of King James
and Queen Anne at
Westminster on 25 July 1603.

The children of King James:
LEFT Henry, Prince of
Wales; the miniature, by
Isaac Oliver, was probably
painted in 1612, a few
months before the
Prince's death.
BELOW LEFT The second son,
Charles, as Prince of Wales;
miniature by Nicholas
Hilliard.
BELOW RIGHT Princess
Elizabeth, who became
Queen of Bohemia after her
marriage to Frederick, the
Elector Palatine, in 1613;
miniature by Nicholas
Hilliard.

the voracious appetite of their public. But a King could not afford to indulge these feelings, particularly one who followed Queen Elizabeth. It was the Venetian Ambassador who pointed the contrast : King James 'did not caress the people nor make them that good cheer the late Queen did, whereby she won their loves : for the English adore their sovereign ... [and] like their King to show pleasure at their devotion ... but this King manifests no taste for them.' Years back, at the coronation of the young Elizabeth, a wise observer had opined that 'in such ceremonies the secret of government doth much consist'. Not only was James an obstinately unheroic figure himself, but he followed the most professional heroine which the stage of the English monarchy had ever supported.

Later James's rather rough and ready Court would become a byword for indecorousness : there was the famous incident of the entertainment of the King of Denmark in 1606. Drunkenness spread even to the ladies, many of whom were to be seen rolling about. Allegorical figures behaved in a manner which ill became the virtues they were supposed to represent : at the mask Hope was too drunk to speak, and Faith staggered away and was found being sick outside. Arbella Stuart, permitted to come to this new Court out of her Midlands seclusion, was amazed to find 'this most ridiculous world' where long-forgotten childish games were played : 'When I came to court they were as highly in request as ever cracking of nuts was.' Anne and her ladies now began to pass their time in 'a continued masquerade', which certainly had more grace about it than the unfortunate Anglo-Danish junketings. But James, although he enjoyed 'such fluent elegancies as made the night more glorious than the day', found his true pleasures in the hunting field as he had in Scotland.

There were marvellous new territories to explore. It was James's passion for the chase, and the country surrounding Robert Cecil's house of Theobalds, that led Cecil eventually to donate it to the King – receiving in return the profitable opportunity to build Hatfield. 'He seems to have forgotten he is King except in his kingly pursuit of Stags to which he is quite foolishly devoted,' wrote the Venetian Ambassador sharply. Later James would be accused of neglecting the affairs of State to gratify this passion.

> Then let him hear, good God, the sounds
> And cries of men, as well as hounds

was the exasperated couplet discovered round the neck of a
wandering beagle, returned to its royal owner. In fact, James
had a quick mind, excellent concentration, and at any rate in
his first years in England could despatch his business quite
quickly if he so wished. Hunting at least animated him with a
proper love of the ancient panorama of English country life.

The truth was that the English, contemplating their Scottish
sovereign, were not only confronted with an alien specimen,
but were themselves embarking on a critical age of transition. A
long and in many ways confining reign had just ended. Opinions
differ and will no doubt continue to differ on whether James's
political problems on the English throne were inherent in the
situation in 1603, leading by inevitable progression to the Civil
War, or whether he, by his peculiar mistakes, helped to bring
it about. But whatever opinion is held, it cannot be denied that
the English themselves, especially the English Parliament, were
at the accession of King James in the mood of horses held too
long in the stable. His remark from Scotland about the tract-
ability of the horse to St George compared to his own unruly
Scottish colt proved to be wildly optimistic. The disciplined
steed of his imagination had perished with or even before the
death of Queen Elizabeth. Something more like a bucking
bronco was waiting for James inside the stable door.

In any case James had very little experience of Parliament on
the English model. In Scotland, he had believed, with justice,
that Parliament could be trained into a useful force to aid the
Crown against the Church or the magnates. In England,
matters were very different. Already the House of Commons,
and in particular its Puritan Members, had shown dangerous
signs of independence and opposition to royal authority;
Elizabeth, with much exercise of energy and charm, had somehow damped these fires down. The arrival of a new and
inexperienced monarch could be a signal for fresh flames to
burn up fiercely and even uncontrollably. This was particularly
true in view of the hold which Parliament claimed to possess
over the grants of money to the Crown. Subject to some
dispute, Parliament was supposed to be responsible for the
legal grant of extraordinary supplies, that is to say, virtually all

OPPOSITE Genealogy by
Renold Elstrack showing
the 'Most Happy Unions'
between England
and Scotland.

Printed coloured and sold by Iohn Garrett at the South entrence of the Royall Exchange in Cornhill going up the stayres

The riotous state of the governors of the nation – a satire on the drunken vulgarity of the Court of King James in the early years of his reign.

direct taxation. Moreover the Crown was heavily in debt at the moment of James's arrival – an unpleasant Elizabethan legacy; he had few personal resources, and possessed a nice penchant for making grants of money and pensions to those around him, notably the Scots who had accompanied him.

In the meantime the procedures by which he was expected to run his finances outside of Parliament were exceptionally inefficient, corrupt, and run down. The household was the chief item of Crown expenditure. Admittedly James, by needing a separate household from the Queen as time went by, and by dividing the Chamber as a special department for ceremonial from the Household, added to its expenses. Yet the point has been rightly made that such display led to prestige as well as insolvency, and as has been seen above, personal criticisms of James lay along lines of his lack of ceremonial rather than abuse of it. Nevertheless, to control his financial situation James would either have to manage his Parliament or bargain with it, probably both. He was ill-equipped by training to do either.

Of course James was gifted with the assistance of the incomparably industrious Cecil, later created Earl of Salisbury. Not all his servants were in the same class of business management. The Howard family, the curse of the next decade, were at this point represented by the Earl of Northampton, who was exceptionally avaricious, and the Earl of Suffolk, who was plainly feeble. In any case, the great families of Elizabethan England have been shown recently to have acquired their wealth by methods less scrupulous than the exquisite appearance of their family palaces would seem to indicate. On the whole this hierarchical society was run by patronage, and was accepted to be so. That could work well or badly for the Crown, depending on the way it was managed and the resources at its disposal. But once again, problems left behind by the last reign remained to bedevil James's potential new deal. James immediately created a 'Multiplicity' of nobles, by which it was suggested that he intended to 'subdue the greatness of the Nobility', make them 'cheap and invalid in the public opinion'. But as Laurence Stone has pointed out, Elizabeth's parsimony had created such a dearth in this respect that it was difficult for James to do otherwise.

James's first Parliament of 1604 was a portent of things to come. There were nagging arguments without settlement over such financially remunerative rights exercised by the Crown as purveyance and wardships. The former enabled the Crown to buy supplies for the royal household at a price selected by the Purveyor, and to command horses and victuals for the royal journeys. The latter was a hangover from the age of feudalism, and entitled the King to the wardships of tenants-in-chief who were minors, including the profitable arranging of marriages for young heiresses. It was irritating to find such a legal right still flourishing, and there were references to an 'obnoxious traffic'. In the end, an influential section of the Commons drew up an Apology, which even if it was not delivered officially, had a sinister ring for the future. It referred to the fact that 'the prerogatives of princes may easily and daily grow while the privileges of the subject are for the most part at an everlasting stand.'

The scope of the royal prerogative was an issue which, though not viewed with clarity at the time and not to be resolved before generations of upheaval, was nevertheless one of enormous significance. Yet James hardly saw it as a problem ; to him the King was supreme in government and law, the fount of justice, was divinely right and could do as he pleased. He would regard the attempted interference of successive Parliaments as dangerous novelties, as had Elizabeth – particularly when they touched on those 'mysteries of state' generally accepted as the sovereign's special preserve, such as the Church, foreign policy and the choice of his own ministers.

But there were those who thought there should be limits to the royal prerogative : they too could cite a whole catalogue of precedents – even if they were usually spurious. Some of the Parliamentarians saw laws enacted by Parliament – statutes – as the highest form of law, overriding, for example, the proclamations of the King. Some of the lawyers, such as Edward Coke, thought that both prerogative law and statutes were only valid if they conformed to that general body of legal precedent inherited through the ages as the common law. One of the troubles was that there was simply no general agreement about which law was supreme; Parliament, when it met, existed alongside prerogative courts like the Star Chamber, Church courts like the High Commission, the Equity Court of the Lord Chancellor and the various common-law courts – all this quite apart from the King himself, proclaiming, suspending, dispensing and also showing mercy by virtue of the prerogative. The root of the difficulty lay in the fact that nobody at this date had any real concept of what it meant to *make* a law at all, since the theory was that true law was *discovered,* hence the scramble to prove that all ideas were justly grounded in precedent. In short, James's case that the Commons were trying to curtail those rights used by Elizabeth was a good one, but it was not the only one. And on this occasion, his disappointed outburst that there had been 'nothing but curiosity from morning to night to find fault with his proposals', was scarcely the most tactful way of handling them.

Perhaps King James would manage England's seething religious situation – which was of course equally an Elizabethan bequest – with more sensitivity. For of all the difficult legacies bequeathed by Elizabeth to her successor none was more intractable, more dangerous, than that of religious disunity. Deep divisions existed within the English Church, even within the English episcopacy. The Puritans – and there were Puritan

Figure of James from
the initial letter of the
Letters Patent,
26 August 1603.

bishops – resented certain aspects of dogma and ritual which
seemed unacceptably close to the practices of Rome; the 'High
Churchmen', or Arminians as they came contemptuously to be
called, were determined to maintain the full panoply of ceremonial, ecclesiastical structure and, most important, to impose
religious conformity. James, however, began with an attitude
of confidence towards these troubles. After all, the middle way
of the English State Church was something very much in
keeping with his own ideas. Experiences in Scotland had made
him tolerant towards those who would show toleration, and

103

also keep the peace. James looked forward to his role as conciliator as to other new and lofty English experiences.

The King had not even reached London when the Puritans presented him with their Millenary Petition requesting him, moderately enough, for such ceremonial changes as shorter services with less music and for a general tightening up on the well-known abuses of pluralism and non-residence. It was not an extreme document, and the new King was not ill-disposed towards it, welcoming the idea of a conference at which he would preside to discuss, and hopefully to reconcile, the matters under dispute between the factions. It was a good start for the Puritans, but as such it horrified the anti-Puritans and, in particular, the powerful traditionalists among the bishops. Men like Whitgift, Archbishop of Canterbury, Bancroft, Bishop of London who was to succeed Whitgift as Primate in 1604, and the scholarly Lancelot Andrewes, were in no mood for concessions. They also hurried to put their own views before the King.

At the Hampton Court conference of 1604 the King was formally asked by the English Puritans to agree to some relaxation of ceremonial. James, thoroughly enjoying the scholarly mantle which such a conference cast upon him, made his own feelings of hopeful compromise clear at the opening. On the first day James said quite distinctly that 'he saw yet no cause so much to alter and change any thing, as to confirm that which he found well settled already; which state, as it seemed, so affected his royal heart, that it pleased him both to enter into a gratulation to Almighty God', at which James doffed his hat 'for bringing him into the promised land, where Religion was purely professed; where he sat among grave, learned and reverend men; not, as before, elsewhere, a King without state, without honour, without order; where beardless boys would brave him to his face'. After these ruminations on the bad old days in Scotland, James repeated that he intended no innovation in the English religion. Yet he had found it necessary to call the conference because of certain complaints 'as in the body of man, corruptions might insensibly grow, either through time or persons'. He intended to be the good physician and examine the body ecclesiastical. Throughout the conference he saw his role as that of chairman, inviting opposing bodies to air their views.

104

Regrettably, on the second day the use of the word presbyter by the English Puritans caused James to identify them more narrowly with his Scottish antagonists than he had done heretofore. The conference also ended without any of the Puritans' hopes being fulfilled; on the contrary, the King declared: 'I shall make them conform themselves, or I will harry them out of the land.' About ninety ministers lost their livings. It was true, as has been pointed out, that Hampton Court was very far from marking a total repudiation of Puritanism in the broadest sense. James himself remained firm in his theological predilection for Calvinism so that its cause in doctrinal terms could not be dismissed during his lifetime. Yet the political consequences of the conference were striking. The failure of the radical Puritans to secure their demands led to them being identified for the future with the party of dissent, while James's political opponents equally turned towards Puritanism. In matters of organisation and administration, James had supported the High Church bishops, and they were to be his allies of the future.

Miniature of King James in the style of Hilliard.

The next violent conspiracy in the life of King James, however, sprang from the disappointments of the Catholics rather than those of the Puritans. James had listened kindly to the pleas of the English Catholics for relief while still in Scotland. Although he himself had no intention of altering his allegiance – later he would say that he was not 'a monseur who can shift his religion as easily as he can shift his shirt when he cometh from tennis' – he did declare that he acknowledged the Roman Church to be the mother church 'although defiled by some infirmities and corruptions': a perfectly tenable Anglican point of view at the time. Once James reached England, he told Cecil that he would be sorry if the Catholics multiplied unduly, yet it was against his conscience 'that the blood of any man shall be shed for diversity of opinions in religion'. Unfortunately Cecil could not be persuaded to allow the relaxation of the laws which the Catholics were now expecting from James. And the King was obliged to assent to even stricter measures against priests and recusants.

The result was an episode known at the time as the Powder Treason, which has gone down to history as the Gunpowder Plot. The genesis of this conspiracy of 1605 can be seen clearly

RIGHT The head of King James on a medal commemorating the peace with Spain, 1604.

BELOW The Somerset House Conference, 1604 at which the Spanish peace was negotiated. On the left are the five Spanish/Flemish delegates; the five English delegates on the right are: (from the window) Thomas Sackville, Earl of Dorset; Charles Howard, Earl of Nottingham; Charles Blount, Earl of Devonshire; Henry Howard, Earl of Northampton; Robert Cecil, Viscount Cranborne. Painting by Marcus Gheeraerts the Younger.

in the saying that 'hope deferred maketh the heart sick'. The Catholics had been led to expect gentler times, and had been met with sterner repression. It was the Jesuit John Gerard who referred to the new anti-Catholic laws as 'the spurs that set those gentlemen [the conspirators] upon that furious and fiery course which they afterwards fell into'. In addition, the peace which James made with Spain in 1604, although undeniably good for the country as a whole, removed from their horizon the possibility of foreign Catholic intervention.

The practical details of the conspiracy are less clear, particularly in the last hours before the official discovery of the plot. It was announced afterwards by the government that a body of Catholic gentlemen, including Robert Catesby and Guy Fawkes, had introduced a quantity of gunpowder into a room close by the House of Lords. Their intention had been to blow it up when it was opened by the King on 5 November. Naturally courtiers and Members would have shared the same grisly fate as the monarch, had not the room been searched on the very eve of the opening, as a result of an anonymous warning letter sent earlier to Lord Monteagle, which he in turn had passed on to Cecil. The gunpowder was discovered in the nick of time; or as Cecil put it four days later : 'And so to have blown up all at a Clapp, if God out of his Mercy and just Revenge against so great an Abomination had not destined it to be discovered, though very miraculously.' The government now took swift punitive action. The conspirators were taken in different ways; some were tortured to confess, including Guy Fawkes himself; Catesby and some others were killed at the moment of capture, that is to say, before they could be questioned. Public executions, of the severe and mutilatory form used for treason, followed. England was left to commemorate the occasion of the King's deliverance annually with the burning of the symbolic figure of Guy Fawkes and the ritual search of the Houses of Parliament by the Yeomen of the Guard on the eve of its opening by the sovereign: which as far as is known has turned up nothing else menacing in the last four hundred years.

But was the discovery of the gunpowder really so miraculous as Cecil declared? Certain circumstances about the plot, notably the strange manner in which the conspirators were able to penetrate the defences of Parliament so easily with their

The Gunpowder Plot:
ABOVE A Dutch engraving of the conspirators and the savage deaths they suffered.

RIGHT The plotters setting fire to barrels of gunpowder beneath the Houses of Parliament.

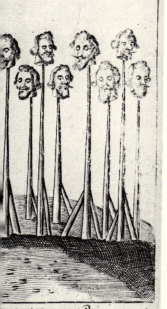

Ihr Anschlag war zu rotten auß
Den König sampt dem gantzen Hauß
Des Parlaments durch eingelegt
Pulfer: der Raht vbel außschlegt
Vnd komt an Tag gar wunderbar
Durch einen Brief der Anschlag gar
Etlich seind in der Flucht erschlagen
Die andre hat man bei der Krage
Genommen vnd in Gfängnuß gstellt
vnd nachdem das vrtheil gfellt
Seind etliche auff Hürden glegt
Vnd zum Galgen hinauß geschleppt
Ein Strick ihn vmb den Halß gethan
Ans Galgenholtz gehencket an
Doch von stundan abgeschnitten:
Auff einer Banck bald in der mitte
Geworffen in ein Fewr bereit:
Das Gottloß Hertz ihn vmb dé Mund
Geschlagen vnd darauff zur stund
Der Kopff abghauwen, vnd endlich
Der leib getheilet in vier Stuck,
Welch hie vnd da seind auffgehangen
Die Köpff gesteckt auff eysern Stange
Vnd offentlich der gantzen welt
Zu einem Schauwspiel furgestelt
Sich das ist der Verrahter Lohn:
So muß auch allen andren gehn

worden

executez a mort. Premierement
continent ostez, puis on les a
... les quartiers pendus

lethal burden, have led to the development of an exactly contrary view. In its extreme form, put forward by Father Francis Edwards, this thesis suggests that the whole plot was a contrivance of Robert Cecil, that Guy Fawkes was an *agent provocateur*, and that a number of his other associates, ostensibly Catholic conspirators, had become double agents at the time of the Essex plot in return for having their lives spared. In this context, the use of gunpowder in what would have been a deliberate attempt to frighten the King, rather than kill him, is significant: for it was gunpowder, as was well known, which had blown up James's father at Kirk o'Field. Cecil did take special care to show the King the mysterious letter of warning in advance, in order to give him the illusion of having interpreted its veiled (but not particularly obscure) message for himself. The trouble with proving this extreme case is that even if Cecil did instigate the plot, he certainly had sense enough and opportunity enough to cover up his tracks afterwards.

There is, however, an important distinction between a plot wholly fabricated by the government and an existing conspiracy

penetrated by their agents. A far more plausible case can certainly be made for the latter : although that again is not susceptible of total proof at this distance of time, with the inevitable erosion of evidence. At least here we are on safer and more familiar ground as regards the working of the English establishment. Very likely the government did know of the plot beforehand, at any rate before 4 November when the search was made, although they had not instigated it. The delay in acting on the Monteagle warning is otherwise inexplicable ; while Cecil's official explanation that he needed time to consult and make inquiries, scarcely holds water if there was any positive danger of a blow-up. It was in the Elizabethan tradition, not long gone, of Walsingham and others to nose out plots, watch over them, maybe even encourage them with a little help from the government's friends, only to uncover them at the last moment. As Bishop Goodman wrote later : 'the very night before the parliament began it was to be discovered to make the matter the more odious...'. Then loud were the government's exclamations of horror and disbelief that such wickedness could exist! At no point, of course, were any real risks taken.

It is James's personal reaction which is our concern here rather than the genesis of the plot, since the charge that he was implicated in any of these double dealings cannot be sustained. For him, the horror of the discovery was only too acute. The man who grew to manhood wearing a padded doublet against the steel of assassinations, whose neurotic fears concerning his safety were the talking-point of his generation, was predictably appalled. He himself drew an analogy with that other threat to his security five years before, the Gowrie Conspiracy, as perhaps Cecil had also intended : 'I may justly compare these two great and fearful doomsdays wherewith God threatened to destroy me.' His conviction of their similarity was reinforced by the interesting fact that both had taken place on a Tuesday and both on the fifth day of the month – 'thereby to teach me, that it was the same devil that still persecuted me, so it was one and the same God that still mightily delivered me'.

At least he did not totally turn away from the rest of the English Catholics as a result, once he had calmed down. The new Oath of Allegiance which was demanded in 1606 did require that Catholics who attended Anglican services should

The gallant *Eagle*, ſoaring vp on high :
Beares in his beake, *Treaſons* diſcouery.
MOVNT, noble EAGLE, with thy happy prey,
And thy rich *Prize* to th' *King* with ſpeed conuay.

A contemporary cartoon showing the miraculous delivery of the Monteagle letter to Cecil just in time for him to warn James of the Gunpowder Plot; woodcut from Vicars's *Mischeefes Mystery*, 1617.

also take the sacrament. But James in fact was less interested in spiritual than temporal supremacy. By demanding that Catholics should recognise their sovereign as their lawful King, repudiating such claims of the Pope as the right to depose heretical princes, James was less concerned to punish them than to develop a more modern theory of Church and State. It was the Pope's temporal powers and governorship at which he was aiming – because they conflicted with what he firmly believed to be his own – rather than his spiritual leadership.

In other ways, James's intellect led him ahead of his times. This quality was displayed not only in his scepticism with regard to superstitions like the King's Evil. He showed an interest in wild animals and their breeding which remind one of the modern movement for conservation, even if his interest in cock-fighting and bull- and bear-baiting was more typical of the age in which he lived. He had an obsession with lions, perhaps because a lion rampant was the symbol of the Scottish Crown, and made them an exercise ground in the moat of the Tower of London where they were housed. There was a nursery to encourage them in the breeding and rearing of young; the King also took an interest in their feeding arrangements, watching mutton and live chickens being fed to them. He even tried the experiment of lion-baiting at the Tower of London, but a lion matched with a bear slunk dispiritedly away.

James also owned the Paris Garden at Southwark, where bears, lynxes and tigers were kept. Here and at the Tower he housed crocodiles, red deer, antelope from India, and a flying squirrel from Virginia. Several presents of tigers were received from foreign princes, and five camels and an elephant from Philip of Spain. The latter grazed peacefully in St James's Park until they were transferred to Theobalds. With zoological interest went also a passion for something in which man could be a more active participant. King James, like many of his descendants, was fascinated both by horse-racing and the breeding of horses. He had a house at Newmarket, where he built one of the several race-tracks for which he was responsible, and introduced some Arab blood to English horse-breeding.

Another of James's preoccupations which has a singularly modern ring was his profound dislike of the tobacco-smoking habit. Or perhaps it would be fairer to say that James simply thought for himself, and as such was inevitably far ahead of his times in some matters. His arguments against smoking issued in his *Counterblaste to Tobacco,* first written in 1604, are in many cases as valid today as then. To the argument that general use proved that tobacco must be beneficial, James gave the telling answer that 'such is the force of that natural Self-Love as we cannot be content unless we imitate everything that our fellows do, and so prove our selves capable of everything whereof they are capable, like Apes, counterfeiting the manners of others, to our own destruction' – which is still the reason why many people first take up smoking in adolescence. As for the problem of smokers married to non-smokers, that was percipiently dealt with: it was an iniquity that 'the husband shall not be ashamed, to reduce thereby his delicate, wholesome and clean complexioned wife to that extremity that either she must also corrupt her sweet breath there with, or else resolve to live in a perpetual stinking torment'.

Of all possible examples, James's plan for an Anglo-Scottish

The Lion rouz'd his floating Mane
in Curls, displays his fired breast,
He rampant breathe forth high disdain,
lift up, and see a stranger Beast,

union was the most far-sighted. It is a matter for real regret that it should have been scuppered by English chauvinism and plain greed : had this proper union been effected so shortly after the union of the two Crowns, some of the worst aspects of Anglo-Scottish relations might have been avoided. James's proposals of 1606–7 displayed that common sense which he had already shown in 1600 when he insisted on beginning the Scottish year on 1 January, like the rest of Europe, in contrast to England who lingered on with a 25 March New Year for another century and a half. All laws were to be framed for the abrogation of any possible hostilities between the two countries. Free trade should be established. All Scots born before 1603 should be naturalised, and all those born thereafter would of course be British.

King James had a great interest in wild and exotic animals, and kept collections of them in the Tower of London and the Paris Garden at Southwark.

ABOVE LEFT A witch surrounded by birds and beasts, some of them imaginary.

ABOVE RIGHT The lion was James's favourite animal, perhaps because it was the symbol of Scotland.

Undoubtedly Brute's descendant had logic on his side in what he proposed, which he believed would lead to 'a perpetual marriage' between the two countries. He also took into account the geographical unity of the island, suggesting that two nations 'under one Roof or rather in one Bed' ought to have complete economic integration. Unfortunately the Scots who had come to England with James had not exactly won all hearts with their rapacity, and James's gifts to Scottish friends had only exacerbated the damage. On the subject of free trade, there was much xenophobic fury. London merchants believed the Scots would first of all benefit from it, and then skip paying their taxes; this could only be avoided if they were under English law, and that meant a union of Parliaments. To this Francis Bacon cited the example of Edward I who had wished to join the two nations together, and James was moved to protest at the number of insults to Scotland expressed in England.

James made an extremely long and eloquent speech on the subject to Parliament. His chief argument rested on the fact that the union had already been made in his person by God, and must now be ratified by Parliament 'so as no splinter may start out'. As to the barrenness of Scotland, Wales was not so fertile as England, said the King, neither were some shires of England as fruitful as the rest. The strength of a country was not in its wealth only, 'but in the Number and Force of Able Men' – an observation on the subject of the Scottish race which the future was to confirm most fully. Yet in the end it was in vain: the scheme failed. The Post-Nati, those Scots born after 1603, did finally get their position legalised as natural born subjects of the English King; but it was only as a result of the collusive Colvill case, and the cooperation of the judges. So the King remained in England, governing Scotland as he put it, 'by stroke of a pen'. It was a pen powerful enough to complete, by 1612, the re-introduction of episcopacy begun in 1600. But an opportunity for unity and rationalisation had been missed.

To these early years belong what many think the *chef d'oeuvre* of King James's work in England, the commissioning of that translation of the Bible sometimes known by his name. The Authorised Version of the Bible was the direct result of James's inquisitive mind, his perpetual interest in the relation of expression to the meaning of things (which might perhaps in

RIGHT The title page of James's *Counterblaste to Tobacco*, published anonymously in 1604. BELOW Smoking scene from Richard Braithwaite's *Solemn Disputation*.

A COVNTERBLASTE
TO *TOBACCO.*

TO THE READER.

S euery humane body (deare Countrey men) how wholesome soeuer, is notwithstanding subiect, or at least naturally inclined to some sorts of diseases, or infirmities : so is there no Commonwealth, or Body-politicke, how well gouerned, or peaceable soeuer it be, that lackes the owne popular errors, and naturally inclined corruptions: and therefore is it no wonder, although this our Countrey and Common-wealth, though peaceable, though wealthy, though long flourishing in both, be amongst the rest, subiect to the owne naturall infirmities. We are of all Nations the people most louing, and most reuerently obedient to our Prince, yet are we (as time hath often borne witnesse) too easie to be seduced to make Rebellion vpon very slight grounds. Our fortunate and oft proued valour in warres abroad, our heartie and reuerent obedience to our Princes at home, hath bred vs a long, and a thrice happie peace : Our peace hath bred wealth : And peace and wealth hath brought forth a generall sluggishnesse, which makes vs wallow in all sorts of idle delights, and soft delicacies, the first

seedes

THE HOLY BIBLE,

Conteyning the Old Testament,

AND THE NEW:

Newly Translated out of the Originall
tongues: & with the former Translations
diligently compared and reuised, by his
Maiesties speciall Comandement.

Appointed to be read in Churches.

Imprinted at London by Robert
Barker, Printer to the Kings
most Excellent Maiestie.

ANNO DOM. 1611.

the twentieth century have led him philosophically towards logical positivism). As early as 1601, with that pedagogic if not academic streak of his, he had urged a new translation on the Kirk. When the matter was raised at the Hampton Court conference, the King responded eagerly : 'I could never yet see a Bible well-translated.' When it came to the method employed for the new translation, James's own suggestion at Hampton Court was, broadly speaking, adopted. The translation was to be made by the most learned linguists in the universities, reviewed by the bishops and other learned churchmen, and then presented to the Privy Council, and finally ratified by the royal authority. It is evident that James's prime motive in his instructions and the care he took in his consultative work, was that the Bible should be easily understood by the ordinary people of the day. For the new Bible was above all an ornament to the English language, over ninety per cent of the words being of English derivation. It was an appropriate gift to his country from the new Arthur.

As a creative artist, James was less successful than as a com- mittee chairman. The revising of the Psalms into a new metrical version he undertook himself. But the King was called to sing Psalms with the angels, as Bishop Williams expressed it felici- tously, before the work was finished. When they appeared in 1631, the Psalms had been supplemented by a great deal of work by Sir William Alexander. In the dedication of the Authorised Version to James, still to be seen in the front of such bibles today, lies the King's true glory :

> Great and manifold were the blessings, most dread Sovereign, which Almighty God, the father of all mercies, bestowed upon us the people of England, when first he set Your Majesty's person to rule and reign over us.

Of these joys none was keener than the continuous teaching of the Word, symbolised by this Bible 'which Your Majesty did never desist to urge and to excite those to whom it was com- mended, that the work might be hastened'. For this reason it is fittingly dedicated to him, 'not only as to our King and Sover- eign, but to the principal Mover and Author of the work'. While the word Author owes something to flattery, the word Mover does not.

OPPOSITE The title page of the Authorised Version of the Bible, 1611.

5

'The Answer
I Expect...'

*The answer I expect : no dutiful
subject can refuse. . . . I have
offered you a bargain, look into it. . . .*

King James

Money, the bane of the Stuarts, was likely to be the cause of the first real clash between King and Commons. Up till now James had been much bedevilled by difficulties inherited from the last reign: it has been estimated that there had been a fifty per cent price rise between Elizabeth's accession and his own, for which the King was scarcely responsible. For the fifty per cent rise in the Crown's disbursements in the initial six or seven years of his reign, he was obviously far more to blame. His extravagant – if generous – nature only contributed to the problems of his office. Of course the parallel extravagance of James's servitors should not be underestimated: the total of Cecil's own expenditure between 1607–12, the years in which he managed to build Hatfield, has been calculated at about £60,000. Lord Suffolk built Audley End which could house the whole Court if necessary. There were other peers like them who profited under the Crown. Ironically, it was easier for those who were battening on the chaotic royal finances to remain solvent, while maintaining their tradition of display, than for the King himself, the fount of all this greed.

Then there were the elaborate masques which were now becoming the hallmark of the Stuart Court. Queen Anne was girlishly enraptured by the possibilities of self-glorification presented by a masque. With Inigo Jones as the instrument by which such delights were brought to life, some exquisite entertainments were enacted. Jones, who had been in the service of the Queen's brother, Christian IV of Denmark, probably returned to England with a letter of introduction to her; by the autumn of 1604 he was working with Ben Jonson on the setting and costumes for *The Masque of Blacknesse*. When Theobalds was handed over to James by Cecil on 22 May 1607, it seems that it was Inigo Jones who planned the display of fantasy on that occasion. Soon masques became as integral a part of Jacobean Court life as the opera was to fashionable Parisian society of the nineteenth century. Inigo Jones, for example, designed that masque in which Henry tilted as Meliadus to celebrate his investiture as Prince of Wales.

But there was more to a masque than mere fertile invention of imagery and scenery. As Roy Strong has pointed out, when Queen Anne was presented as Bel-Anna, Queen of the Ocean, or King James as Pan, the universal god, or Prince Henry as

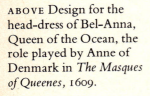

ABOVE Design for the
head-dress of Bel-Anna,
Queen of the Ocean, the
role played by Anne of
Denmark in *The Masques
of Queenes*, 1609.

RIGHT Drawing by
Inigo Jones for the
costume of Oberon played
by Prince Henry in Ben
Jonson's masque
Oberon, 1611.

Oberon, Prince of Faery 'a deep truth about the monarchy was realised and embodied in action'. They were deliberately exposed before the Court in roles which expressed 'the strongest Renaissance beliefs about the nature of kingship, the obligations and perquisites of royalty'. Under King James, the Office of Works became a source of great patronage as the Crown once again entered the lists of the builders, from which Elizabeth's economical nature had kept it long removed. It has been estimated that over £75,000 was spent between 1607 and 1611.

From 1615 onwards Inigo Jones was made Surveyor to the Crown and under his presiding genius the great Banqueting House, which still survives, part of a vanished Whitehall complex, and the Queen's House at Greenwich, were initiated. In the Banqueting House, the majestic decorations were intended to lead up to a climax of the King himself sitting in state, and it thus represented the final apologia of a King turned to a God. Here at last was the throne, and the god-like style of *Basilikon Doron*, recreated on earth. Unfortunately long before the God-King's earthly throne was established (in the next reign), the God-King's troubles with his unruly subjects had become notorious : there was no question of his putting his new godhead to proper use. Such is ever the gap between art and experience.

Quite apart from extravagance, James allowed himself to become lazy. He took the line, said the Venetian Ambassador, quoting the old tag, that since God had given him the Papacy in the shape of the English Crown, he was determined to enjoy it. Whereas in Scotland his incisiveness had increased as the reign progressed, in England, whether for reasons of health or age or both, it turned out that the graph of his concentration was shaped more like an arc. Sooner or later, there would be a downward slope.

It was relevant to this that his homosexual tendencies, for whose origins in the deprivations of his childhood a sympathetic cause has been pleaded, now took a more dangerous form. This was the political power accorded to James's new Scottish favourite, Robert Carr. In Scotland the favourites, Lennox, the first love, the proud and bullying Arran, had at least proved bastions for the King against the rest of the aristocracy. In England, there was nothing like the same evident need to bolster up the Crown which looked from the outside strong enough. To put it at its lowest, Lennox and Arran had needed to build up royal authority if only to implement their own positions. Carr, and later the still more disastrous Buckingham, saw the Crown as a sort of old-established and utterly secure cornucopia from which benefits for themselves and their families would flow in a happy and endless stream. It never occurred to them, neither being men of any particular political perception, that they might actually damage the source of their bounty. It was not within their capabilities to think that far ahead.

James brought with him the political perception, but unfortunately he was quite convinced that the King of Great Britain must be a rich man, where the King of Scotland had been a poor one. As to the indignation of those nobles, heads of the ruling families, who considered themselves the King's 'natural councillors' and as such unfairly excluded by upstarts such as Carr and Buckingham, it did not occur to James that such a dangerous emotion needed careful handling. Perhaps their indignation was unjustified and merely self-centred, the traditional outrage of those who have enjoyed a good thing for so long that they consider it to be their right – 'We was robbed.' But the general vagueness of the constitution at this time at least permitted them to hold that point of view. Whether selfishly or not, they were certainly correct to feel themselves threatened by the favourites. James, however, lived happily in a cocoon of his own ideas in which the King had an absolute right to choose his own counsellors.

The first of the fatal favourites, Robert Carr (the English spelling of the name), was twenty years younger than the King. He was the younger son of the Scottish family, the Kerrs of Fernihurst, and astonishingly good-looking: 'fierce and gentle like the swift greyhounds of Teviotdale, which doubtless is a parish in Fairyland', said a lyrical contemporary. His first introduction to Court (still in Scotland) was not auspicious, for as a royal page he made such a mess of reading the Latin grace that he was dismissed. His second introduction went better, perhaps because it was more romantic. On 24 March 1607 he caught the King's eye at a tournament, offering his patron's shield to the royal box. Shortly afterwards Carr broke his leg.

Riding at the quintain, from illustrated instructions
in the art of riding and jousting. Tournaments were
a popular form of entertainment during the reign of James
and it was at such an occasion that his fateful
involvement with Robert Carr began.

It was a case of *Felix Culpa*! Charing Cross Hospital, to which he was carried, became the scene of a right royal romance, as the King fussed over the sick-bed of his new beloved like a mother (or father) hen, jealously trying to beat off the rest of the courtiers. The latter, never slow to take this kind of hint, thronged round with inquiries which may have been kind but were not exactly disinterested. 'Lord, how the great men flocked to see him then,' wrote the malicious Sir Anthony Weldon, 'and to offer to his shrine in such abundance.' Praise of Carr became the regulation route to James's favour: 'Will you say that the stars are bright jewels fit for Carr's ears?' asked another sarcastic onlooker of this new obsequiousness.

Was the King's relationship with Carr, or indeed with Buckingham later, actually consummated? The aptest comment on the subject would seem to be that of Thomas Osborne. Describing the lascivious kisses which James was prone to give his young favourites in public, he said that people wondered what might not be done in private. James has had his defenders, on the grounds that nothing was done in private just because there was so much pinching and fondling in public. In sexual matters, however, it is generally better to assume the obvious, unless there is some very good reason to think otherwise. In any case, it is an academic argument, for the degree of their intimacy is less important than its political consequences. What is certain is that Carr's rise to fame and fortune was rapid. He became Viscount Rochester in 1611 and Earl of Somerset in 1613 – he was the first Scot in the English House of Lords. He was also enabled to become a very rich man by James's indulgence, and at the time of his marriage was rumoured to have spent £90,000 within the last year.

Unfortunately Carr was neither intelligent nor modest enough to act in a manner which would have made this patronage less disastrous. At the height of their love James taught him Latin – that Latin he had once mutilated when saying grace: another courtier commented savagely that it would be better if someone taught the jumped-up Scot to speak English properly. Later, in decline, Carr turned out to be a hysterical scene-maker: 'I shall never pardon myself but shall carry that cross to the grave with me, for raising a man so high as might make him presume to pierce my ears with such speeches,' exclaimed poor James in dismay. In his hey-day, Carr's most outstanding quality, on which all contemporaries agreed, was insolence.

In 1610 James's new need of Parliament turned not only on money: it also touched those nebulous areas of the English constitution where Parliament was tacitly admitted to have its rights. It was true that the King claimed in theory divinely granted rights, which if exercised, would have directly excluded those of Parliament. The fact was that in practice King and Parliament were felt by both sides to be linked together, as a director, playwright and actors are linked in the production of a play. But as in the theatre, the apportioning of power could be the subject of much nagging argument, particularly in the event of failure. King James throughout was confident that he was making concessions unheard of to previous monarchs. He told the Commons that unlike any other Prince before, he intended to offer 'retribution i.e. a bargain which was without example'. 'The answer I expect,' he said, 'no dutiful subject can refuse. I plead. I have offered you a bargain, look into it, and then to what you as dutiful subjects shall present me, it will become me to give you an answer.'

This bargain, this offer which James thought his subjects could not refuse, was known as the Great Contract. It was fundamentally the work of the beaver-like Cecil, since 1605 Earl of Salisbury, and since 1608 Lord Treasurer, after the death of Dorset. The King, he was supposed to have said, 'would no more rise and fall like a Merchant'. In fact, Salisbury by sweating and labouring for the King's relief, in James's own phrase, had increased the revenues of the Crown. The debt stood at £600,000 at Dorset's death, due to the excess of expenditure over income, which had to be met by royal borrowing, generally at ten per cent, with disastrous results. But there was also a rise in customs' receipts after the Spanish peace of 1604. Salisbury sold some Crown lands to try to make ends meet. Other methods were more dubious, such as the imposition of extra customs duties. Although this resulted in Bate's case of 1606, in the end the Court of the Exchequer decided that the King was within his rights. Foreign commerce was regulated by the King's prerogative, those special powers of the King beyond his powers when acting in Parliament: so the new impositions were not illegal. One way and another, by 1610 the income of the Crown had gone up to over £350,000.

The trouble was that James was still encumbered by a deficit of about £130,000 and a future expenditure likely to amount to £600,000. Parliament was the answer. There must be some more prudent solution to his problems than this perpetual state of crisis. Was it for this that he had taken the prosperous highroad from Scotland? 'I could rather have wished with Job never to have been born than that the glorious sun of my entry should have been so soon overcast with the dark clouds of irreparable misery,' said the King. He talked of his estate and his honour lying a-bleeding 'for to require help of his people and be denied were a disgrace both to him and his people'. Speed was the essence of the game: 'the longer delay we made, his necessity would be the greater and *qui cito dat bis dat* – who gives quickly, gives twice.'

When the details of the Great Contract came to be hammered out, however, it seemed that the Commons were more likely to give slowly, and give half of what was expected. The lower House was in a difficult mood. There were problems of royal technique: Salisbury, elevated to the Lords, was no longer there to manage it; James did not understand the use of the Privy Councillors in the Commons in order to keep it tractable and too many of his Councillors were now in the Lords. The Commons had evolved an anti-monarchical device called the 'Committee of the whole house', first used in 1607. This so-called committee could elect its own chairman; it could also sit as long as it liked, and members could speak more than once; all this represented an advance of Parliamentary freedom in an age when the Speaker of the House of Commons, unlike today, was a royal nominee. The Commons offered £100,000 for the abandonment of wardship alone. James wanted twice as much. In the end £200,000 was offered for the abolition of wardship, purveyance and other concessions, while the royal aids were to be restricted to £25,000 a year; and the possession of an estate for sixty years was to be sufficient title against the King and his heirs.

Parliament was prorogued, but at the reassembly of the House, the Commons showed that they had not finished with the King. They were clearly bent on further discussions of the

OPPOSITE The Marble Hall at Hatfield House, looking towards the Minstrels' Gallery; on the right is a portrait of Elizabeth I by Hilliard, at the far end a portrait of Mary Queen of Scots by Oudry. Robert Cecil acquired the old royal palace of Hatfield in exchange for his house, Theobalds, to which James had become attached. Between 1607 and 1611 Cecil built a vast new mansion for himself, a hundred yards from the old palace.

128

Si. Paſſ: ſculp: Aº 1612.

Are to be ſoulde by Compton Holland. ouer
againſt the Exchange at the ſigne of the Globe.

King's extraordinary financial measures, his right 'by his prerogative royal, without assent of parliament, at his own will and pleasure, to lay a new charge or imposition upon merchandises', as Hakewill had put it earlier. James on the other hand asked for the immediate grant of a large sum which would pay off his debts. He was enraged by the discussion of his prerogative, for debating the impositions, which were levied by use of the prerogative, was tantamount to debating the prerogative itself. At this the Commons took the line that the King was trying to interfere with their right of free speech. James's words, wrote John Chamberlain, 'bred generally much discontent to see our monarchical power and royal prerogative strained so high....' There were furious denunciations of the Scottish favourites in the House. James, in disgust, first adjourned and then dissolved Parliament. The Great Contract, the King's unheard-of bargain, was at an end.

The subtle undermining of the system by which Elizabeth had managed Parliament was beginning to show its consequences. James could offer little of the personal charm and zealous blandishments employed by England's former Deborah. It was especially ironic that it was about now, according to Bishop Goodman, that men began to look back to Deborah's reign, she who had understood so well how to keep them in a kind of bondage. At first 'the people were very generally weary of an old woman's government', and memories of Elizabeth's habit of wailing 'I am a miserable forlorn woman' had endeared James to them. But, 'after a few years, when we had experience of the Scottish government, then in disparagement of the Scots, and in hate and detestation of them, the Queen did seem to revive; then was her memory much magnified.' In short, so began that love affair of the English people with the legend of Queen Elizabeth which has continued ever since. Like all legends, it has blinded them to much reality, including the fact that not everyone necessarily shares it: the English have never understood, for example, why the Scots do not like to regard the present Queen as Elizabeth II, but more accurately in their own terms as Elizabeth I.

In contrast to the Virgin Queen, James at this point had a young family, with all that implies of joys, sorrows and responsibilities. James loved his children. His eldest son,

OPPOSITE Prince Henry with the pike; a famous rendering of the popular, athletic prince who died tragically in 1612.

131

Drawing of a masquer by
Inigo Jones for Thomas
Campion's *The Lords'
Masque,* performed
before the Court on
14 February 1613.

Prince Henry, looked more like Queen Anne, with perhaps a touch of his grandfather Darnley's good looks. He reacted buoyantly against his father's intellectual preoccupations, as many eldest sons do: 'I know what becomes a Prince,' he exclaimed. 'It is not necessary for me to be a professor, but a soldier and a man of the world.' The lamentations after his premature death in 1612 – 'both for wisdom and strength of body there was not the like to be found among the English' – may have given an exaggerated account of Henry's qualities: Francis Osborne said that the people were making 'their common mistake, who think all such virtues lost in the untried dead'. But in the suggestion that he had a most gracious smile and a terrible frown, one gets a hint of a youth who understood already the art of being royal. The English were probably right to mourn him, in view of the perplexing character of James's remaining son, Charles, then aged eleven.

The marriage in 1613 of James's daughter Elizabeth fell primarily into the pattern of his foreign policy. Against new friendship with Catholic Spain was to be balanced his daughter's alliance with the Protestant Elector Palatine. It was however characteristic of the revival of sentimental feeling for the previous reign that many comparisons were made between the two Elizabethans, one dead but glorious, the other young but full of similar promise. Shakespeare's *Henry VIII,* of roughly the same date (1612–3), concluded with a speech by Cranmer prophesying the dazzling rule of the infant Elizabeth in the presence of her father Henry. There were flattering references naturally to James in this chorus of Elizabethan nostalgia: the old Queen was to be the 'maiden phoenix' from whose ashes another heir:

> Shall star-like rise, as great in fame as she was
> And so stand fix'd; peace, plenty, love, truth, terror ...
> Shall then be his, and like a vine grow to him:
> Wherever the bright sun of heaven shall shine,
> His honour and the greatness of his name
> Shall be and make new nations ....

In 1613 this was perhaps a somewhat over sanguine picture of James's achievements: but no doubt the King enjoyed the Bard's dramatic licence.

Reality was rather different. The ceremony itself was marred on the one hand by the King's melancholy – he was still prostrate with grief and illness over Henry's death – and on the other by munificent display which the nation's finances could ill afford. The prettiness of it all lay in the appearance of the youthful bride and bridegroom: Elizabeth, in a dress of silver tissue, with her hair hanging down her back to signify her maiden state, was surrounded by youthful attendants in white satin. She wore 'an exceeding rich coronet' on her head, which James next day rather tactlessly valued at a million crowns; the crown jewels were also on show, including 'the fair great pearl pendant called the Bretherin, the Portugal Diamond, and the great table diamond set in gold called the Mirror of France'.

Yet it must have been rather depressing for the young couple to find that in Westminster Abbey the effigy of Elizabeth's dead brother Henry 'as he went when he was alive' was still on view. And when the Elector Frederick was made a Knight of the Garter, James, with his usual instinct for ruining State occasions, managed to forget to dub him. Sitting up in bed, the King simply slung the George round the young man's neck 'after a few words'. At the wedding itself, James showed that indifference to his own appearance which he never lost, being as John Chamberlain described it, 'somewhat strangely attired in a cap and feather with a Spanish cape and a long stocking'. Then James complained about the boredom of the infinite celebrations which followed: although his financial plight might have made it preferable not to have indulged in them at all, having indulged, he might at least have enjoyed himself. Modern taste is even more outraged by his subsequent attitude to the young couple, for immediately after the wedding night, he decided to visit 'these young turtles that were coupled on St Valentine's Day and did strictly examine him [the sixteen-year-old bridegroom] whether he was his true son-in-law and was sufficiently assured'. In short, the wedding of James's beloved Bessy did bring out that faintly ludicrous side in his public behaviour which his rather pathetic curiosity towards the sexual relationships of others only enhanced.

It was more dignified that, in September 1612, James had the coffin of his mother transferred to Westminster Abbey from Peterborough Cathedral where it had lain since her execution.

Adspicis exiguâ illustres in imagine vultus,
  Magna Palatini scilicet ora ducis :
Qui superat magnis teneros virtutibus annos,
  Et quoque magnanimos nil nisi spirat avos.

Crisp: Pass: fig: sculp: et excudit

Bucheli. tu.

Frederick V, Elector Palatine, who married James's daughter Elizabeth on 14 February 1613. Frederick was elected King of Bohemia in October 1618, an event which helped to precipitate the Thirty Years' War.

OVERLEAF Frederick with his entourage landing at Gravesend on his way to London to marry Princess Elizabeth.

There it was interred in a magnificent monument begun six years earlier, when it was put to James that the memory of the mother of the sovereign needed to be honoured. In this Northampton, a secret Catholic, was largely instrumental. Another relic of the past, Lady Arbella Stuart, had been allowed to remain at Court, where it was thought easy to supervise her, but she was not permitted to marry. As long as James's children were still young, the marriage of such a close relative as Arbella could present a threat. Arbella was to be a compulsory Virgin

135

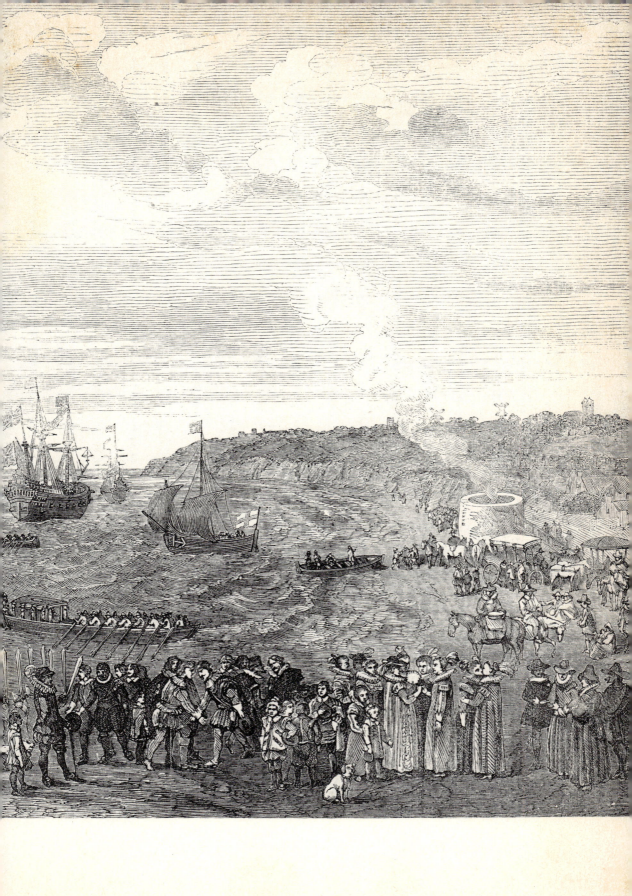

Lady, where Elizabeth had been a voluntary Virgin Queen. James showed cunning in his treatment of Arbella, whereas his poor cousin, in her imprudent elopement with another semi-royal cousin, William Seymour, showed nothing but Stuart foolishness. Imprisoned for her behaviour, she eked out her days in prison till her death. A popular ballad referred to her correctly as 'Fair Arabella child of woe', and a privately composed epitaph pointed to the source of her sufferings, her position in the royal family tree: 'And what my birth did claim my death has paid.' Arbella died in 1615, aged forty, and was laid appropriately enough inside the new tomb which James had just had constructed for his mother.

More in keeping with James's own natural bent than the visual splendour of a white marble tomb, were his efforts to defend his mother's memory in prose. He did not ask the historian William Camden to rewrite his *Annales* as has sometimes been suggested, but he did ask Camden to defend the memory of Mary Queen of Scots against the attacks of the French historian Jacques Auguste de Thou. De Thou had made use of Buchanan's writings and James made Camden send him a list of Buchanan's errors. In Camden's own *Annales* he followed James in rejecting Buchanan, and blaming representatives of the Scottish aristocracy, Moray and Morton, for the whole of Mary's misfortunes. Camden ended on a cosy note in which the hand of King James can be detected more surely than the feelings of Mary Queen of Scots: 'Queen Mary (as she said even at her death) desired nothing more ardently, than that the divided kingdoms of England and Scotland might be united in the person of her most dear son....'

It was natural that James, who in his published works had posited such a definite theory of royalty, should take the posthumous reputation of one royalty so closely related to him seriously. Jacobean drama, from which the notion of royalty beleaguered or magnified by praise was never far absent, was also of course patronised by the King. Ben Jonson referred to the sweet Swan of Avon, and his flights upon the banks of the Thames. *The Tempest*, if not performed at the actual wedding of Elizabeth, centred its plot on her marriage. But apart from *Henry VIII*, Shakespeare's flights in James's reign consisted even more prominently of the great tragedies: *Macbeth,* for

139

example, was intended as a double tribute to a Scottish monarch and an expert on witchcraft. Both *Othello* and *King Lear* were put on at Whitehall in the presence of James. David Mathew points out that whereas John Webster's *The White Devil* was referred to in 1612 as acted by the 'Queen's Servants', *The Duchess of Malfi* was recorded in 1623 as having been performed publicly at the Globe by 'the King's Majesty's servants': from this change, some aspect of patronage at least by 'our James' can be deduced. In any case he believes that in the play itself, and particularly in the central character, we approach 'the very essence of the Jacobean world in its court angle'. When the ill-fated Duchess exclaimed in the famous passage:

> Why should only I
> Of all the other princes of the world
> Be cas'd up, like a holy relic?

did she perhaps allude to that hieratic state, sprung from divine right, with which James fondly imagined that his subjects saw him surrounded?

James's relations with scholars on the other hand were uneven: as might have been expected from one who considered himself the great schoolmaster of the realm, James was not always happy with those who set themselves up as rivals. Much to James's credit is his patronage of John Donne. James praised Donne and made him chaplain in ordinary. Subsequently he commanded Donne to attend a dinner at which he promised to carve him 'of a dish that I know you love well'. The dish was St Paul's – of which Donne was made Dean. But John Selden, with whom James had three disputatious meetings, had his history of tithes suppressed. Still worse from the point of view of a writer, Selden was commissioned to produce a pamphlet for the King to answer the Dutch doctrine of freedom of the seas, and in the end that too was suppressed for fear of annoying the King of Denmark. The College of Heralds fared better from his patronage, and James was interested in the idea of an Academy Royal to hold lectures 'of heroic matter and of the antiquities of Great Britain', as well as a possible college in Virginia for helping Indian children. The Society of Antiquaries on the other hand, which had hoped for a revival under his auspices, failed to get it.

LEFT Miniature of Robert Carr, Earl of Somerset, in the manner of Nicholas Hilliard, *c.* 1611.
BELOW The Tower of London, *c.* 1615; painting by a Dutch traveller. Carr and his wife were imprisoned in the Tower in 1616 as a result of their involvement in the Overbury scandal, and were not released until 1622.

De Toutr van London aen de Refierre Legende 1615 346

THE TRAGEDY

OF THE DVTCHESSE
Of Malfy.

As it was Presented priuatly, at the Black-
Friers; and publiquely at the Globe, By the
Kings Maiesties Seruants.

The perfect and exact Coppy, with diuerse
things Printed, that the length of the Play would
not beare in the Presentment.

VVritten by **John Webster.**

Hora.——— *Si quid*———
———*Candidus Imperti si non his vtere mecum.*

Jo: gatos

LONDON:

Printed by NICHOLAS OKES, for IOHN
WATERSON, and are to be sold at the
signe of the Crowne, in *Paules*
Church-yard, 1 6 2 3.

BELOW John Donne, poet and divine. In 1615 he became Chaplain to James, and from 1621 to 1631 he was Dean of St Paul's.
BOTTOM Ben Jonson, poet and dramatist. He was the author of many of the masques performed at the Court of King James.

OPPOSITE The title page of John Webster's *The Duchess of Malfi*, first published in 1623.
BELOW The title page of the First Folio edition of Shakespeare's plays, 1623, with the portrait by Martin Droeshout.

Mr. WILLIAM
SHAKESPEARES
COMEDIES,
HISTORIES, &
TRAGEDIES.
Published according to the True Originall Copies.

Martin Droeshout sculpsit London

LONDON
Printed by Isaac Iaggard, and Ed. Blount. 1623.

FIDEI DEFENSOR · POTENTISS IACOBV · D·G·MAG·BRITANI

Icy dans ceſe chambre coũtena
nostre Roy Iaques premier de nom
le 27 ^{me} d'oust
1615

University visits would obviously be to James's taste and he made expeditions to both Oxford and Cambridge. A jaunt to Oxford in 1615 went particularly well : the King described the Bodleian Library as a garden from which the fruits of the university sprang, and was inspired to the further flight of fancy, by the sight of the founder's bust, that he should be termed Godley, not Bodley. If he were a captive, said King James, he could imagine no better prison than the Bodleian (or Godleian) Library. Some characteristic Oxford experiences were to be had : a lot of wine was drunk, a supper was held at Christ Church, the undergraduates became intoxicated, and during some of the plays James fell asleep. In 1615 he visited Cambridge, around which an aura of Puritanism had hung, to the King's disquiet. Cambridge responded by wondering anxiously whether James's visit to them would be as drunken as his visit to Oxford. And in the end the King still seems to have preferred Oxford to Cambridge, because Oxford's reception of the Latin edition of his works in 1619 was thought to be more gracious. In Scotland, James considered himself the godfather of Edinburgh University, on account of the founding charter he had granted it in 1582. In 1617 he decreed that it should be known as 'King James's College'. Although 'a royal God-bairn gift' for enlarging its patrimony never actually materialised, it is true that he confirmed its privileges in an Act of 1621 and placed it on an equal footing as the other Scottish universities.

In another outlying quarter of the British kingdom, a university was more financially fortunate. James did settle a pension upon Trinity College, Dublin, payable upon the Irish Exchequer, and endowed it with large Ulster estates. But the consequences of James's Irish policy were in other and greater ways not so happy. King James had a chance in Ireland, if ever any British monarch could be enlightened enough to solve its problems. In England, Elizabeth had left him a Parliamentary wasps' nest. But in Ireland, the rebellion of the chiefs had been crushed, the Earls Tyrone and Tyrconnell had fled, and the Anglo-Spanish peace, in addition, freed him from the ever-present fear of Catholic invasion there. At the wedding of James's favourite Somerset, four Irishmen brought on to the stage spoke a ridiculous jargon, intended to represent the dialect of the country. The sentiment :

OPPOSITE Stained glass window with a portrait of King James dated 1615.

King James giving his works to the University of Oxford and to Fame; statue on the Tower of the Five Orders of Architecture, Old Schools Quadrangle, Bodleian Library, Oxford.

This is that James of which long since thou sung'st
Should end our country's most unnatural broils

had more to commend it. Unfortunately the policy which James thought most suitable to ending Ireland's most unnatural broils, that of plantation, turned out to be that most likely to prolong them.

'We intend nothing with greater earnestness than the plantation of Ulster with civil men well affected in religion shall be accomplished with zeal and integrity,' wrote James in 1609. Money as well as piety played its part in these calculations: by giving two-fifths of the forfeited lands to English and Scottish settlers known as undertakers, it was planned that the Crown would be enriched. One-fifth went to the needs of the Church and education. That left a comparatively small amount for the native Irish who had been there in the first place. In the south, James's principal aim was to incorporate the Catholics into the

146

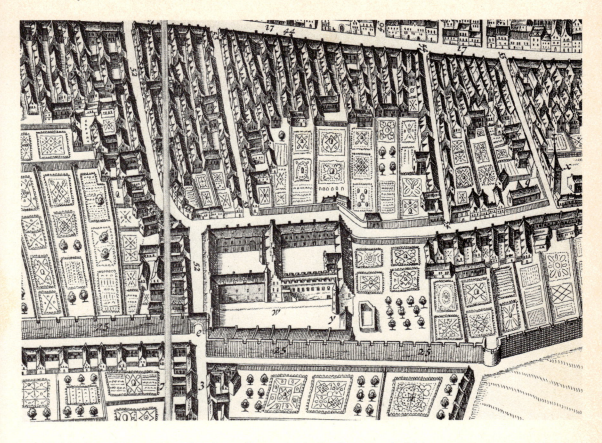

English Church. As a result, the solitary Irish Parliament held during his reign, that of 1613–15, was largely occupied in endless bitter arguments. Like the policy of plantation, James's religious dictates showed little appreciation of the nature of Ireland itself or of Irish conditions. Neither in his attempt to eliminate Irish feudalism, nor his plans for the integration of the Catholics, did James get the answer he expected, the sort of answer he told the House of Commons no dutiful subject could refuse. On the whole it is pleasanter to concentrate on his good record with regard to Trinity College, and to realise, charitably, that King James was merely one of a long series of British sovereigns and leaders who had not the faintest understanding of the history, hopes and fears of the Irish people.

A bird's eye view of Edinburgh University, granted a founding charter by King James in 1582.

6
Spaniels and Wolves

He 'spared not great personages about the court calling them arrisores et arrosores, *which he Englished spaniells to the King and wolves to the people.'*

Comment on the Addled Parliament of 1614

The portraicture of Robert Car Earle of Somerset Vicount Rochester, Knight of the most noble order of the Garter &c. And of the Ladie Francis his wife

ROBERT CECIL, EARL OF SALISBURY, died in 1612, worn out perhaps by his massive efforts to put the King's finances on the right road. James did not at first appoint a new Secretary, although Francis Bacon offered his services, and was so convinced that he would become Master of the Wards in Salisbury's place that he put his men into new cloaks. When Sir Walter Cope got the place, it was said Sir Walter was Master of the Wards, and Sir Francis of the Liveries. Bacon, who, at fifty-one, was already curiously old for the start of a career in the royal service, subsequently became Attorney-General. In the meantime James, if he could survive without a Secretary, found that he could not survive without a Parliament.

The genesis of this new Parliament of 1614, was to be found as before in money. But the course of its proceedings is best summed up by the fact that James hoped that it would be called the Parliament of Love, whereas it has gone down in history as the Addled Parliament, one by which not a single act was passed. Like the previous Parliament, it would break down in frustration and bitterness, with the King determined not to sacrifice his own theories of the 'prerogative royal' on the one hand and Parliament equally determined on the other not to donate subsidies without some discussion of this crucial subject. Various reasons for this failure have been sought. It used to be suggested on the authority of Bacon that the trouble lay with the high proportion of new Members. But T. L. Moir's detailed study of the Parliament revealed that, although inexperience was at the root of the King's difficulties, it was the inexperience of his advisers and managers, not the inexperience of the Members, which hampered him. How James would live to regret the death of his 'little bossive Robin' – for Salisbury understood the art of management not only from a lifetime of study and industry, but also because such knowledge seemed to be acquired by osmosis from the very air which Cecils breathed. When James did appoint a Secretary of State he chose a man put forward by the favourite Somerset, Sir Ralph Winwood, who had never actually taken his seat before. The Speaker of the House himself had not sat in the House for twenty years.

It was true that the opposition was not particularly homogenous, and indeed the very word is anachronistic, if it is

Charles Howard, Earl of Nottingham, one of the many members of the influential but corrupt Howard family. He was Lord High Admiral during James's reign until Buckingham took his place in 1618.

thought to convey a solid organised party in the modern sense. There could be no named opposition, since now and right into the crucial years of the 1640s it was officially treason to oppose the King. From the first there was more danger of a stalemate (without a subsidy) than of some radical solution. After all, James could at least count on the House of Lords, and not only because those Privy Councillors who were vanishing from the Commons, with dire consequences, had fetched up there. Out of the eighty-four lay peers, over one quarter had been created by James, and still others had had their ancient titles restored. The Howard family, whose cancer-like hold on James's administration was to prove a feature of this decade, was firmly installed in the Lords.

The Howard clique had recently received a potent addition to their number in the shape of Somerset. Basically, in politics at least, the Howards, including Lord Nottingham, the Lord High Admiral, as well as Northampton and Suffolk, represented the pro-Spanish interest which had been rising since the peace of 1604. In contrast to the anti-Spanish party, including the Lord Chancellor Ellesmere, Archbishop Abbot and Lord Pembroke, this interest found much favour with the King. In personal terms, as will be seen, the Howards represented rapacity and aggrandisement to an extraordinary and disastrous degree. This revelation lay ahead. At the present time, it seemed like a master stroke, or the completion of a great family arch, when Frances Howard, one of Suffolk's numerous daughters, achieved a marriage to the favourite Somerset.

Frances Howard was unquestionably extremely seductive: even her enemy Arthur Wilson described her as 'a beauty of the greatest magnitude in the horizon of the Court ... every tongue grew an orator at that shrine'. She was also wilful and spoilt, and like some people who have been indulged from youth, had a certain crude impatience in attaining her ends. At the age of thirteen she had been married off – unwillingly – to the young Earl of Essex. One can sympathise with her in refusing to make do with the groom whom she had seen only once, and her subsequent infidelity, including a brief spell as the mistress of Prince Henry, was at least explicable. But once her sights were set on Somerset, and Frances realised that matrimony to the

THE SECOND PART OF VOX POPVLI,
or
Gondomar appearing in the likenes of
Matchiauell in a Spanish Parliament,
wherein are discouered his treacherous & subtile Practises
To the ruine as well of England, as the Netherlandes.
Faithfully Translated out of the Spanish Coppie by a well-willer
to England and Holland.

Simul Complectar omnia.

Gentis Hispanæ decus

Count Gondomar, the wily Spanish ambassador at the Court of King James, portrayed as Machiavelli in T. Scott's anti-Spanish pamphlet, *Vox Populi*.

prized favourite was within her grasp, she showed an unbecoming ruthlessness.

For Frances was determined to secure a proper annulment of her marriage to Essex, and for this she needed to secure nullity *propter frigiditatem,* i.e. on account of the total impotence of her husband towards all women, rather than *propter maleficium versus hanc,* which meant that he was simply impotent towards her personally. To have pleaded the latter reason would have been both kinder and truer, as it seems unlikely that the unfortunate Essex was ever allowed to essay his capacity towards Frances: she probably resisted consummation from the start.

154

As it was, Essex's reputation was sacrificed. James weakly allowed undue pressure to be brought, so that the precious annulment should be given and Somerset should wed his Frances. As one contemporary wrote 'the holy state of matrimony was made but a May game'. It was for the new wedding that John Donne wrote that exquisite poem praising 'those wombs of stars, the Bride's eyes'.

> First, her eyes kindle other ladies' eyes
> Then from those beams their jewels' lustre rise ;
> And from their jewels torches do take fire ;
> And all is warmth and light and good desire.

Later those famous bright eyes would also bring death.

James's second Parliament opened on 5 April 1614, with a long procession, including knights, baronets, judges, peers and bishops, like so many chess-pieces. The King came at the end, wearing a crown and riding a horse, followed by Somerset leading another horse. There were the usual ridiculous incidents. One bishop fell off, at which he was mocked by a Puritan lord ; then he too fell off and broke his arm ; the Catholics were left laughing that both their adversaries had been discomfited. Another feature of James's philo-Spanish feelings was his friendship with the Spanish Ambassador Sarmiento, later Count Gondomar : this lively quicksilver Spaniard understood exactly how to amuse James, now speaking bad Latin to make him laugh, now accompanying him gamely out hunting. On this occasion James would not set out until the Spanish Ambassador was ready, which aroused the scoffing of the crowd ; the Spaniard was later installed in a privileged position in the House of Lords behind a silk curtain with holes in it to give a secret view of the proceedings. These began with James's speech, in which he touched on religion and the need for a measure of tolerance towards the Catholics. There should be a revision and enforcement of existing penal laws, rather than new laws, he said, for if Protestantism was the true religion it could not fail to succeed and supplant Popery. What religion, true or false, had ever gained properly by persecuting its enemies ? These admirable sentiments were less the matter of his speech than its ending, in which he asked the Commons to give him the much needed finance. He disclaimed any intention of extending his prerogative : he hoped that it might be done out of love.

But love proved to be in short supply. The Parliament, said John Chamberlain, turned out to be more like a cockpit than a grave council; many of the MPs were more fit to be among the roaring boys than in that assembly. One of the most significant of their attacks, and the Commons grew every day 'more fiery and violent in their speeches', was that on Richard Neile, Bishop of Lincoln. Neile had declared in the House of Lords that the Commons ought to accept the impositions as a legitimate part of the royal prerogative : argument was seditious. But Christopher Neville, younger son of Lord Abergavenny, denounced the Court for its corruption, calling the ruling clique *arrisores et arrosores,* which he put into English as 'spaniells to the King and wolves to the people'. There were many further wild speeches before the King gave up in despair and dissolved Parliament. This had long been the preferred solution of the pro-Spanish party. Since some of the later speeches aroused in James a fear that his enemies intended to assassinate not only his Scottish favourites but himself, it is possible that these outbursts were indirectly inspired by the Howards. No acts were passed by the Addled Parliament, but four of the most outrageous members were imprisoned.

James's theory of his place in the constitution has been neatly contrasted by Alan G. R. Smith with the theory of his Parliament about that place in two statements of 1610. James postulated that 'Kings exercise a manner or resemblance of Divine Power upon earth', whereas James Whitelocke had put forward the counter view that 'the power of the King in Parliament is greater than his power out of Parliament and doth rule and control it'. To this fundamental debate, which would not be settled before the Civil War, the Addled Parliament contributed nothing in particular. The Parliamentary opposition was not sufficiently developed to do more than protest. Contest would have to wait for later. In the meantime James retreated towards that expedient which his son Charles would try at even greater length, personal rule of the sovereign without Parliament. The next assembly would not be called for seven years, the longest gap without a Parliament since the Reformation. And then it was mainly occasioned by external circumstances which had little to do with the King's own desires.

But, of course, the royal financial crisis had not been solved by the *débâcle* of the Addled Parliament. The death of the Lord Treasurer, Northampton, added further chaos to the looming possibility of bankruptcy. The bishops came to the rescue and offered some plate; some of the aristocracy proffered cash; money was raised by benevolences from the City, although not as much as had been anticipated. Suffolk succeeded his uncle as Treasurer: to the proverbial incompetence and confusion of the royal accounts, he now added irregularities which amounted to outright dishonesty. Indeed, Suffolk conducted his personal finances in such a way that irregularities were almost built in to the system. He had already derived enormous profits from farming the customs, which had been let to him at advantageous rates through the benevolence of Salisbury. His obligations to the customs farmers were such, as Laurence Stone has pointed out, that 'it would have been wholly unreasonable to expect him to have exercised judicial objectivity in his official negotiations with them'. Far from being 'the plain honest gentleman' of James's imagination, Suffolk subordinated public interest to private gain to an unsurpassed degree, his only justification, if that be considered one, being the needs of his vast family of children. Bribery and scandals in the awarding of contracts became a commonplace, adding a further stench to what was already the rotting situation of the Crown's finances. Just as James leaned towards Spain, believing that a marriage of his heir Charles to the Infanta Maria would balance the Protestant marriage of his daughter Elizabeth, so Suffolk echoed the King's hopes in his own materialistic fashion by receiving the charity of the King of Spain.

Some of the most vociferous of James's critics in the Addled Parliament had been the lawyers, who had constituted quite a high proportion of its members. Part of James's problems with the common lawyers sprang from his inability to appreciate fully the nuances of English common law, which was after all very differently based from that of Scotland. At the same time, just as new theories of Parliamentary rights were being put forward, similar new ideas concerning the force of the common law were beginning to be expressed. A crucial figure in the development of this notion of the supremacy of common law was Edward Coke, who in 1606 had become Chief Justice of the Court of Common Pleas. Here he worked hard to try and

HOLLAR

restrain the various prerogative courts such as that of the High Commission. The King, he held, could not change the law merely by proclamations. Later, as Chief Justice of the King's Bench, Coke maintained that the judges should not be consulted separately, either privately or publicly, but only as a body. The Peacham case of 1615 brought Coke into direct conflict with the King on this point. Oliver Peacham, a clergyman, had been committed to the Tower the previous year for having written (but not preached or published) a sermon

ABOVE An early seventeenth-century drawing of Westminster Hall with the Courts of Chancery and the King's Bench in session. The judges are sitting under the canopies; lawyers can be identified by their long gowns with wide sleeves.

158

ABOVE RIGHT Sir Edward Coke.
In 1606 he was appointed Chief Justice
of the Court of Common Pleas and
subsequently clashed with the royal
authority.
RIGHT Sir Francis Bacon, philosopher,
essayist and statesman. He became Lord
Chancellor in January 1617, but four
years later was brought down by his
enemies on charges of corruption
and bribery.

159

attacking the King's governing. By this time James was bene-
fiting from the adept advice of Francis Bacon who, unlike Coke,
believed that judges should be 'lions, but yet lions under the
throne, being circumspect that they do not check or oppose any
points of sovereignty'. Bacon counselled James to avoid Coke's
dominating influence by appealing to the judges one by one on
the legal questions arising out of the Peacham case.

A case of commendams in 1616 brought the final clash.
James had granted a living to the Bishop of Coventry and
Lichfield *in commendam,* i.e. to be held along with his own
preferment. When a case brought against the Bishop in respect
of this living was being argued in the Exchequer chamber
before twelve judges, James used Bacon to send a message
saying that further action should be stayed until the royal
pleasure was known through consultation with the King. His
point, once again, was that his prerogative was being attacked :

> ... it was a fault in the Judges, that when they heard a counsellor
> at the bar presume to argue against his Majesty's prerogative
> [which in this case was in effect his supremacy] they did not
> interrupt and reprove sharply that loose and bold course ...
> especially since his Majesty had observed that ever since coming to
> the crown, the popular sort of lawyers have been the men that most
> affrontedly in all Parliaments have trodden upon his prerogative.

The other judges succumbed, but not Coke, who was eventually
dismissed. In terms of the past, rather than the future, there was
more to be said for James's contention in the Star Chamber that
it was 'presumption and high contempt in a subject to dispute
what a king can do, or say that a king cannot do this or that',
than Coke cared to admit. In any case, some of Coke's claims
for the common law also cut across that supremacy of statute in
which some Parliamentarians believed. Once again, as with the
Commons, James was unlucky in his moment of arrival in
England.

James's Court, for all Bel-Anna's fantasies, had never been
much admired by the populace. But now its moral degeneration was pointed out in the most unpleasant public way, at a
peculiarly unfortunate moment for the royal image, by the
poisoning of Sir Thomas Overbury; both Somerset and his
wife Frances were supposed to be heavily implicated. The
Overbury murder has none of the detective-story fascination of

Those Swan-like notes, sung so insurally
to thy untimely fall, prove most exact
Limes drawne from Life; & ths swift Tragedie
showes but thine owne Soules Prophecie in Act.
Thy Name, and Vertues live: To kill the Mould
was all Imprisonment, and Poyson could

But the more-heavenly-Self, from double Baines
sett free (at once) thy free Body, and the Tower,
In that Supreme-uncertaill Court remaines,
Fear, nor Ambition, Envy, Lust have power:
Redeem'd from poysonous riotts, from Witches Charmes
from Westons &c to Apothecaries harmes. W. B.

Sir Thomas Overbury,
murdered by poison in the
Tower of London;
engraving by
Renold Elstrack.

those earlier mysteries in which James had been involved. It is a squalid tale. The victim had been an ambitious man who, from writing poetry and enjoying the friendship of Ben Jonson, and something more intimate with Sidney's daughter the Countess of Rutland, had graduated to a valuable intimacy with Somerset. As the favourite's confidant, he was described by Weldon as Somerset's Pythias. But Overbury had made the mistake of strongly opposing the marriage to Frances, fearing to see the influence of the Howards replacing his own with the volatile

162

Somerset. He had failed to calculate the odds in favour of the marriage correctly, so that once Frances had secured her prize, Overbury found a ready-made enemy in the new wife. Imprisoned in the Tower of London, Overbury was gradually poisoned by a series of disgusting jellies, one or two of which, not being consumed, turned green before the eyes of horrified observers. Frances's guilt seems certain, not least because she had had previous associations with poisoners, Somerset's innocence equally assured.

Nevertheless at the trial which followed, for all that Frances cut a poignant figure in black 'with cobweb lawn ruff and cuffs' and made a great show of penitence, both Somerset and his wife were condemned to death. The King commuted the sentence to life imprisonment and so the unhappy pair were left languishing in the Tower. But as so often happens with a *cause celèbre,* the damage spread far beyond the principals : a whole way of life was on trial, that of King James and his favourites. It was the King himself who was the real sufferer. How could the reverence which the English loved to feel for their sovereign be directed towards one who had been involved, however peripherally, in this unsavoury mess?

In subsequent centuries, one of the most damaging weapons used against the ageing King has been the pen portrait of Sir Anthony Weldon. He gave an all too vivid picture of James slobbering over his male favourites – although the tongue which was too big for his mouth and caused him also to spill food and drink was an accident of his unhappy birth, and therefore deserved sympathy rather than contempt. James's skin, wrote Weldon, was as soft as taffeta sarsnet, because he never washed his hands, only rubbed his finger ends with a wet napkin; he walked leaning on other men's shoulders (another relic of his crippling birth) 'his fingers ever in that walk fiddling about his cod-piece'. It is interesting to note that this evocative sketch, which has successfully blackened King James in the common imagination, was not actually available to his contemporaries but was first published a generation later, in 1650 in the republican atmosphere of the new Commonwealth. It should also, in fairness to James, never be quoted without the important rider that Weldon had been excluded from Court circles and had in consequence a pathological

hatred of the Stuarts. Weldon has certainly had his revenge for the slight injuries done to him.

All this lay in the future. What was important in King James's lifetime was his guilt by association in the whole sordid Overbury affair. It was true that James had not been involved in any practical way with the imbroglios of Frances and Somerset, except to help on unwisely the Essex annulment. But it seemed that no spoon was long enough to sup with the greedy and amoral Howards.

Quite apart from the Overbury scandal, their days were already numbered; it was fitting that the Howard regime should wane, as it had waxed, in the light of a royal favourite. The new luminary, George Villiers, was probably deliberately introduced out of the general desire, excepting the Howards, to get rid of the insolent Somerset, 'one nail [as the proverb is] being driven out by another'. In any case, Somerset had to contend with that old rule of love in the words of Bishop Goodman, that 'a man be glutted with one favourite, as he is feeding upon one food, though it be manila, therefore a choice of dishes best pleaseth the palate'. Villiers first met the King in 1614 and his progress may be charted by his social rise: he was knighted in 1615, Earl of Buckingham in 1617 (the year after the Overbury trial), Marquess in 1619 and Duke in 1623.

Originally Villiers was considered 'a modest and courteous youth' but that proved a remarkably false picture, for there was never anything modest about him, and once he had achieved power, nothing particularly courteous either. Like other favourites he insisted that his family rise with him, which might show a nice nature but proved hideously expensive for those who had to foot the bill – the government. Originally his dependents had so little of grace about them that special country dances had to be ordained at Court for their sake. Soon the little Villiers children were running up and down the King's lodgings 'like rabbit-starters about their boroughs'. James also, in his patriarchal way, came to love the Villiers women – anything, so long as he had his George.

What were the qualities which inspired the King's last and most disastrous love? He also gave it out to be his greatest love, although that is the sort of defiant statement which it is tempting to make in old age, when it is sad to think that the greatest

A satire on the medical profession: a quack administers a purge from a flask labelled wisdom, while from the chimney rise strange chimeras which make the recumbent figure mad. The satire is probably connected with the Overbury scandal since the fashionable lady and gentleman show a great resemblance to the Earl and Countess of Somerset.

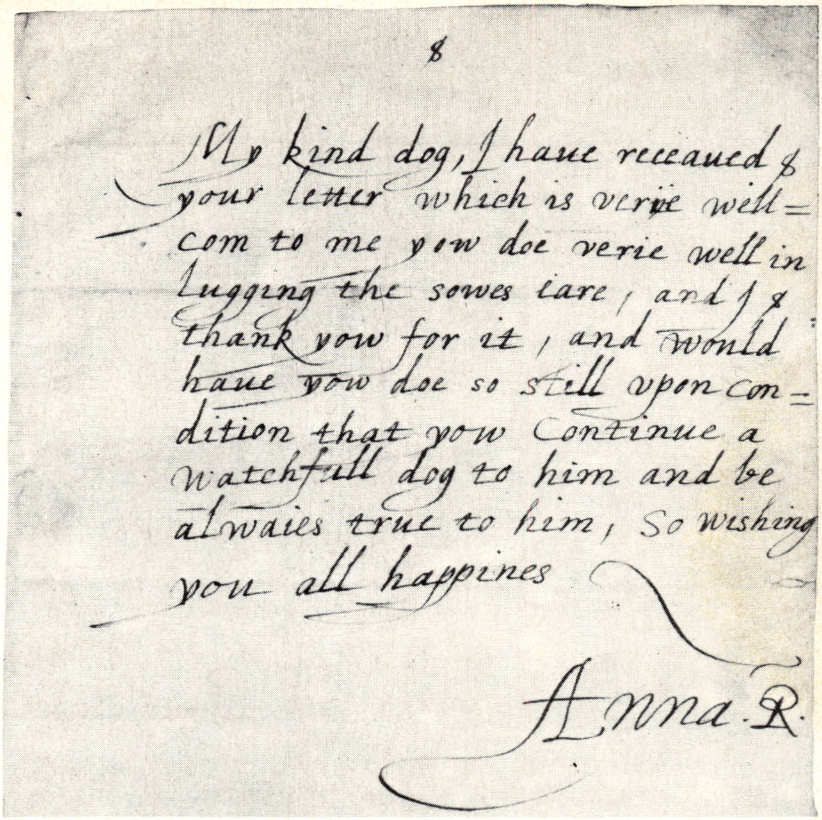

8

My kind dog, J haue receaued of your letter which is verie well-com to me yow doe verie well in lugging the sowes eare, and J thank yow for it, and would haue yow doe so still vpon con-dition that yow Continue a watchfull dog to him and be alwaies true to him, So wishing you all happines

Anna R.

RIGHT Letter from Anne of Denmark to Buckingham beginning 'My kind dog . . .'.

OPPOSITE Letter from James to Buckingham in Spain. It ends: '. . . god blesse thee my sweete Steenie and sende thee a quikke and happie return with my sweete babie, in the armes of thy deare dade and stewarde.'

love may lie in the past. James's language about Buckingham was certainly extravagant; it was also pathetic. He told his Council in 1617: 'Jesus Christ did the same and therefore I cannot be blamed. Christ had his John and I have my George.' Buckingham was 'his only sweet child'; his 'sweet child and wife'. Thus the language of fatherhood became mixed with that of sexual love, as James signed himself 'thy deare dade' and 'thy deare dade and stewarde'. Buckingham's attraction was obviously strongly physical: with his dark eyes and chestnut hair he intoxicated the King and he had that combination of beauty and strength which the Greeks had admired in young men. But there was something more to Buckingham, a sort of ebullience and *élan,* which led him to mad unpredictable exploits, only enhancing his charm in the eyes of the doting King. In short, Buckingham was dashing. It was sad that he was also arrogant, greedy and corrupt, so much so that those who had brought in the new nail would even live to regret the old one.

168

My sweete Steenie thow remembers, that among
manie other particulairs guhairof
I gaue thee an accounte in my last letre to thee, by
grisley, I tolde thee, that mylldmie hadde putte
me in hoape that the east indien cumpanie wolde
presente thee with twelf hundreth poundis
sterling, but I fownde he huntid upon so colde
a sent, as thy best stewarde was forced to laboure
in it, him selfe, & now I can assure thee, thaye
will presentlie presente thee with two thousande
powndis & deliuer it to thy wyfe as thy nea
rest freende, & so god blesse thee my sweete steenie
& sende thee a quicke & happie returne
with my sweete babie, in the armes of thy deare
dade & stewarde.   James R

bromane the last of iulie.

LIONEL CRANFIELD EARL
OF MIDDLESEX LORD HIGH
TREASURER OF ENGLAND

Before extravagant Buckingham grasped the reins, the galloping horse of the royal finances had actually had its pace stayed a little. The emergence of Lionel Cranfield, originally an assistant to Northampton, as the King's chief financial adviser marked a period of hopeful reassessment. By 1615 a new policy of rationalising the tariff had actually increased the royal income by £30,000 a year. Cranfield held the sound philosophy on the subject of James's resources that whatever payments had to be made out of them, they should at least not diminish his future revenues. Assignments on the revenue should therefore be loans, not gifts. By 1617, it seems likely that James's Household expenditure had risen to well over twice that of the last years of Elizabeth; the Household was said to be nearly £20,000 in debt, and the Wardrobe nearly £70,000. Cranfield was determined to discover if by adopting the excellent motto: 'the King shall pay no more than other men do', he could actually abate this ruinous flood of increase. When he analysed expenses in 1618, he found that over 2,000 oxen and veal, 13,000 sheep and lambs and nearly 19,000 dozen hens and chickens had apparently been devoured. In June 1618 James agreed to a new deal, by signing Cranfield's regulations for the management of the Household. Cranfield now ran the Wardrobe on an average outlay of £13,000 from 1619–21, whereas the King had been previously paying out £28,000. Although, as all economisers do, Cranfield aroused opposition, he pointed out with spirit that he had not abridged anyone's diet, but 'only their stealing and thieveries'. These figures indicate the justice of his claim.

In the navy, scandalous speculation, bribery and waste were discovered. Nottingham, the Howard Lord High Admiral, was sacked. Everywhere, it was found, the depredations of the Howards had spread like a trail of vicious mice, destroying what they could not consume. The inefficient Exchequer was one thing, but when the accounts of Suffolk, the Howard Lord Treasurer, were found to be gravely wanting, he too was removed from his post in the autumn of 1618. Suffolk was accused of embezzlement and his wife of taking bribes. As a result of their submission before trial, the Suffolks were fined £30,000 and ordered to return all monies wrongfully extorted. When Cranfield became Master of the Court of Wards, the current receipts were increased by over a quarter.

171

It must be admitted that Cranfield, like everyone else in this period except King James, who had no opportunity to do so, was busy feathering his own nest, in the sense that his personal assets increased over three-fold between 1611 and 1620. Had not even Cecil netted £25,000 out of the Treasurership? But Cranfield did have a firm grasp on the true needs of the Crown, that government departments should have their staff cut for example, and that an absolute veto was necessary on further alienations of the royal lands. He even suggested a capital levy on one year's income for anyone who had in any way enjoyed James's all too liberal bounty. James had grown even more generous with old age, donating pensions wildly, and he absolutely refused to have them cut by a third as Cranfield wished. Nevertheless he was on surer ground financially by 1620 than he had been in either of his kingdoms before. It is possible that he might have lived to enjoy the kind of royal solvency which would have obviated the need of calling obstreperous Parliaments for many a long year. But he was threatened by three forces over which he had no control. One was the developing state of affairs in newly seething Europe. The second was that Trojan horse inside his Court, Buckingham. The third was old age.

Per Bellum, mihi Pax

Cinge Gladium

Da Cæsari.

Miserere

Some there are that find such fault with your Majesties government, as they wish Queen Elizabeth were alive again, who (they say) would never have suffered the enemies of her religion to have unbalanced Christendom, as they have done within these few years.

Tract c.1622

7 Unbalanced Christendom

THE KING WHO HAD TO COPE with the problems produced by the outbreak of the Thirty Years' War in Europe was no longer young either in years or in fact. James was now fifty-four, not a great age by modern standards, but mature by the standards of his own time. It has been further suggested that James was what we would term 'a bad fifty-four'. Ever since James arrived in England, he had in one sense been relaxing, stretching out before the fire of English warmth, as one who had come in from outside, from the tough Scottish years. To this psychological attitude, that of the man arriving out of the wilderness in the King's own phrase, was now added the physical handicap of failing health. As a result many historians have taken the line that after 1614 James was not so much old as senile.

King James was additionally reminded by the death of Anne of Denmark in 1619 of those long fingers which must in the end touch all mortals. They had not shared even a household for ten years, and the King's superstitious dislike of such things kept him away from both her deathbed and her funeral. But he was cast into a great melancholy by her death in spite of spinning some consoling verses :

> She's changed, not dead, for sure no good prince dies
> But, as the sun sets, only for to rise. . . .

Then James became extremely ill, and in agonies, was said by his doctor to have passed three stones.

To this picture of steady degeneration the researches of Robert Zaller, showing that even in 1621 James could display skill in his handling of his problems, are a welcome corrective. Nowadays the question of James's health must also be bound up with the recent researches into porphyria, dubbed by Doctors Ida Macalpine and Hunter, 'the royal disease'. It therefore seems relevant that while porphyria weakens and incapacitates, it also provides periods of temporary recovery. Porphyria generally appears in adolescence, takes the form of sudden attacks associated with abdominal pain and local nervous symptoms, including rheumatic pain and mental disturbance ; attacks increase as the patient ages. In their analysis of the health of James's direct descendant, King George III, the doctors have come to the conclusion that he must be diagnosed

PREVIOUS PAGES
'The Revels of Christendom', an anti-Papal satire.

OPPOSITE The ceiling of the Banqueting House at Whitehall painted by Rubens in Antwerp and delivered to London in 1635. The centre panel represents the apotheosis of King James; he is supported by Justice and Religion, while above him are Victory and Wisdom (in the shape of Minerva) bearing a laurel.

not as a manic-depressive but as a porphyriac. Tracing its course backwards – since porphyria is a hereditary disease along Mendelian lines – they have made a case for King James suffering similarly if less severely.

In many ways, James's medical symptoms, as recorded in great detail by his physician, the celebrated and meticulous Theodore Mayerne, represent what has been termed 'a description of porphyria in all but name'. The King suffered from attacks of colic, vomiting and diarrhoea, which were preceded by moods of depression, as well as weakness and spasm of the limbs, and a fast and irregular pulse. The convulsions which caused his death would fit into the porphyriac pattern. He also had the ultra-sensitive skin of the typical sufferer from porphyria of the variegate variety, thin and fragile, itching and sweating easily, and easily subject to bruises (hence the rubbing of the hands with taffeta sarsnet mocked by Weldon). His skin was especially sensitive to sunlight, and suffered from over-heating if given undue exposure to it. His urine was from time to time the purple colour of Alicante wine – Mayerne's comparison – and although Mayerne at the time diagnosed haematuria due to a stone in the kidney, this purple colour is yet another characteristic of porphyria, from which the name is actually derived. Above all, there is an attested connection between mental stress and some of James's collapses. The dissolution of Parliament of 1611, the death of Prince Henry, these were followed by prolonged bouts of illness.

Of course there are problems with any medical diagnosis given at such a distance of time, in the absence of the patient or a proper autopsy. And in general consideration of Doctors Macalpine and Hunter's thesis about porphyria, medical sceptics have emerged, in particular those who have had experience of modern sufferers of porphyria: these have not been convinced that sufficient numbers of patients of royal descent have been brought forward to display the necessary Mendelian pattern. Until Doctors Macalpine and Hunter produce that evidence, it is fair to regard their overall case as not yet 'proven'. Nevertheless, while the argument continues, the existence of Mayerne's astonishingly realistic notes does seem to justify a tentative diagnosis of porphyria in James I. In that case we are faced with a patient who will show signs of

OPPOSITE An emblematic representation commemorating the death of Queen Anne in 1619. She is portrayed lying on her tomb, with her head resting on Jacob's Stone. Her spirit is seen on the top rung of the ladder to heaven.

178

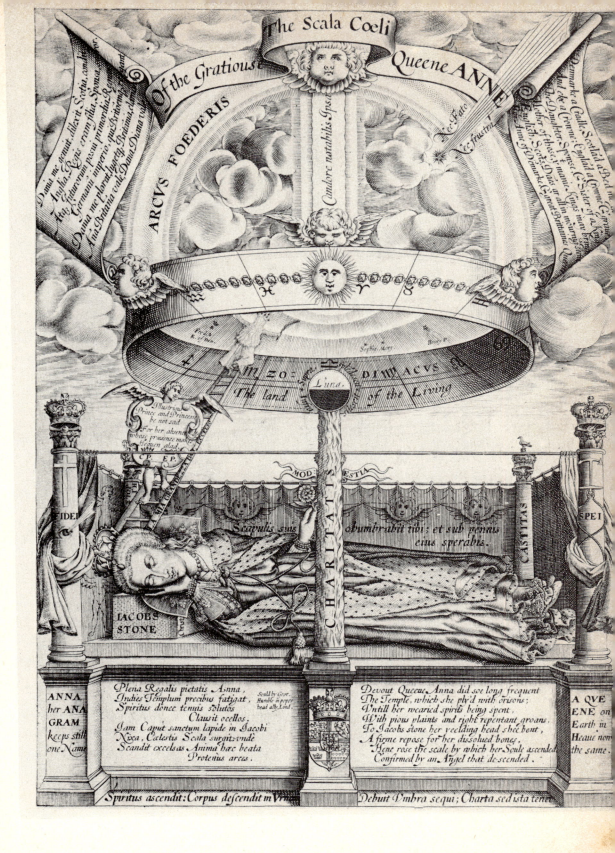

Drawing of Sir Theodore Turquet de Mayerne by Rubens. Mayerne was a celebrated French doctor who came to England in 1606; he was physician to James I, Charles I and their consorts.

mental disturbance which could be interpreted as senility, but only intermittently.

Certainly the old man who trailed north to Scotland in 1617 was very different from the cheerful energetic Scot out to enjoy his new fortune of fourteen years before. Yet it was the King's obstinacy alone which succeeded in pushing through the necessary preparations for the visit. His English advisers begged him to eliminate such quite unnecessary extravagances as a tour of his northern kingdom. Buckingham also voted against the plan, but on this occasion at least the King snarled at him, so that the favourite was 'glad to run away'. It was true that the measures needed for his comfort and that of the Court justified the contemporary description of the expedition as 'a very costly voyage in every way'. Not only tapestries and silver, but even such small luxuries as melons and cherries had to be sent north, such was the King's passion for soft fruit. Leaving aside the expense – and all Court progresses and indeed all journeys were expensive in the seventeenth century – King James was surely justified in insisting on his 'salmon-like' visit to the land of his birth. His concept of Britain, where Scotland at last had its place, was in refreshing contrast to the complaints of his courtiers dragged away from English sophistication. On the subject of his solitary Scottish visit it is difficult not to share the sentiments of William Drummond of Hawthornden:

> Ah why should Isis only see thee shine?
> Is not the Forth as well as Isis thine?
> Though Isis vaunt she hath more wealth in store
> Let it suffice thy Forth doth love thee more.

In Scotland, James took the opportunity of his visit to hunt happily round Falkland and in Perthshire, as well as receiving some flattering deputations in Edinburgh, and admiring a statue of himself at the Nether Bow. He found a country already displaying signs of economic progress, and still marked in the main by that peace and order which he himself had striven to institute. He also, of course, pushed forward his determined de-Puritanisation of the Scottish Church. The Five Articles of Perth of 1618 imposed those Anglican rituals on the Scots such as kneeling at communion, and the celebration of the Christian festivals, which were to cause such trouble to James's son Charles I. But James, in securing assent to the Articles, at least showed political cunning. Having first won over the ministers by increasing their stipends, he then proceeded to threaten those who refused agreement with the removal of the increase. Scotland could still be managed by a King in person who understood the country. Charles in the 1630s would present the face of the absentee landlord who also knew little of the ways of the tenantry.

James's English Puritans, one way and another, caused him more trouble. Given his own theories of kingship, James had no real choice in throwing in his lot with the High Church bishops as he had done early in his reign. It was true that he suffered from grave misgivings concerning their political wisdom and issued warnings to his son – alas, unheeded – on the subject: he refused for example to promote Laud. Yet it was the High Church bishops who had embraced the principle of Divine Right; they were the chief opponents of the Presbyterian element among the Puritans; Church money was needed when the King was in

King James on horseback on an English silver coin. On the caparison of the horse is a crowned thistle.

financial difficulties; above all the bishops were part of the hierarchical structure of church government of which the King was the head.

Choice or no choice, the alliance was a fateful one with political as well as religious consequences. For religion and politics were inseparable. The King was head of both Church and State; the bishops often officers of State as well as of the Church. Through his bishops and priests the King had the support of the greatest propaganda organ known to the seventeenth century – that of the pulpit. The clergy could, and did, preach on the obligations of loyal subjects to pay taxes as well as on their obligations to God. In these circumstances it was not surprising that just as James's political opponents were branded as religious dissidents – Puritans – they in turn labelled the High Church extremists as Papists. Here James's well-meant leniency towards his Catholic subjects, his pro-Spanish foreign policy, and his support of the Episocopal establishment all combined to give his opponents a powerful propaganda weapon of their own. As a developing theme, this polarising of political and religious attitudes was a momentous one, which, when the time came, was to prove a disastrous legacy for Charles. In matters of detail, it led to continuous aggravation.

For example, in contrast to the triumph of the Five Articles, James in the same year, in England, had to issue the *Book of Sports,* in order to check the Puritan practices which were demolishing the pleasures of the sabbath. The avowed aim of the Book of Sports was to protect 'dancing, playing, church-ales', delights now laid down as permissible on Sunday once church was over. It declared that the prohibition of sports on Sunday bred discontent, hindered the conversion of Catholics and deprived the 'commoner and meaner sort of people' of their only opportunity for proper recreation and physical exercise 'seeing they must apply their labour and win their living in all working days'. These excellent arguments for a freer Sunday still seem good today, when our laws continue to prevent the British workforce from enjoying its day of relaxation in the manner of its own choice. But of course King James himself was less concerned with popular pleasures than the diminution of the political influence of the Puritans.

Such were the preoccupations of Puritans and their opponents

The pleasures of alcohol illustrated in two drinking scenes, depicting the aristocracy and artisans. In the *Book of Sports* issued by James in 1618, drinking church-ales was one of the pleasures permitted on Sundays.

in James's own time. To a later age, however, Jacobean religious dissent is probably far more famous for the voyage of the Pilgrim Fathers in the Mayflower in September 1620 than for any other single event. In the same way King James himself worried over Scotland and the union of the two kingdoms: but a far more striking fact about the period of his rule to our own eyes must be the effective founding of the British Empire. At the beginning of James's reign, there were no British colonies: at the end a quantity would already have come into existence. England's long contests with Spain had made her a late comer in the colonial stakes. But after the Anglo-Spanish peace of 1604 she

183

POWHATAN
Held this state & fashion when Capt. Smith
was deliuered to him prisoner

MONACANS

POWHATAN

MANGOAGS

CHAWONS

THE VIRGINIAN SEA

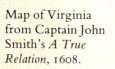

VIRGINIA

Maſſaw: Omecks

Maſſawomeck

Tanxſnitania

Hasni:uza

AHOACKS

Mahaskahod

Tauroteck

Qumen

opeck

stawomo

Pataromerk

titan

Pamesack

 men

Rickahone

Mamahunqunt

Tauxenent

Nuſhemouc

Pamacook

Petapaco

Cinquoteck

Namaſſunathem

omeck

Moyaons

Aſſaomeck

Naſ:inraughquend

Teſſamatuck

Wighcocomoco

Weſtanco

Nacotchtanck

Moyumpſe

Kattymuni

Quatataqun

Pamuroment

Rickahocke clifes

N

A

Cepowia

Attaock

Teſſinogh

Quadroque

PEACK BAY

Powhls Iſle

Bornes point

Ozinio

Poynt Peſune

Cockpowh flu

Saſquoſahanough

Kuſkarawaock

Kerchmynd

omeck Iſ

ARAWA

OOKS

Nantacmack

TOCK

WOGHS

Pergorens mount

Quikrawaock

and halfe

e of Lea gues

Leagues

Chickahokin

Atquanachuke

Macocks

LVKES

The Saſqueſahanougs
are a Gyant like peo ple &
thus a tyred

Vechowic

SASQVE
SAH
OVGH
AVQ
ANAC

ABOVE Drawing by John White of a fortified Indian village. White's drawings and writings about North America in the late sixteenth century did much to arouse interest and encourage settlement in the New World during James's reign.

RIGHT Captain John Smith, captured by the Indians, is rescued by Pocahontas. Smith, the most famous of the early settlers in Virginia, had many narrow escapes from disaster during the few years that he spent there trying to encourage colonisation.

186

King Powhatan comands C.Smith to be slayne, his daughter Pokahontas beggs his life his thankfullnes

was free to enter into the fascinating sphere of colony-founding : here the treasure-hunting economics of the State mingled with private-enterprise efforts to found fortunes, and the desire for religious freedom was only one element in this interesting hotch-potch. James himself believed genuinely that no form of conquest was so easy and so innocent as that of plantation (it was a policy he had also preached towards Northern Ireland). He also observed with much truth that Scotland was well adapted to plant colonies, since a colony required the exportation of men, women, cattle even and victuals – but not money.

Apart from the Pilgrim Fathers' settlement starting from their landfall at Plymouth, plantations were set up or attempted in Massachussetts, Bermuda, Newfoundland, Guiana, the East Indies and India. Then there was the royal colony of Virginia, an example of private enterprise and hopeful fortune-hunting ; in this James has been described as taking 'a more than nominal' interest. When Spain protested against the settlement, the King responded robustly, defending Britain's right to colonise. His first patent to the Virginia Company of 1616, and his instructions for the government of the colony, indicated his intention of taking considerable care over its future. And although he abandoned royal control in the charters of 1609 and 1612, James continued to pepper the colony with good advice. They should plant hemp, fruit and vines, anything rather than the hated tobacco. Above all, they should plant mulberry trees to feed silkworms, in order to promote a silk industry. James, in Virginia and elsewhere, showed a fascinating obsession with silkworms. He planted mulberry trees in the gardens at White-hall, and the royal silkworms were granted special attendants as well as a groom of the Chamber whose task it was to carry them 'whithersoever his Majesty went'. But there seemed to be a sort of curse on those silkworms destined for Virginia, for they never actually reached it : some were shipwrecked in 1609, and others died at sea on their way there in 1622. Virginia tobacco of course was another story, although not one of which King James could ever have approved. In 1624, just before his death, the King did dissolve the Virginia Company : but his principal motive was the need to reduce the colony from the angry chaos into which it had fallen, rather than something more sinister.

OPPOSITE Sir Walter
Ralegh with his son.
Ralegh spent most of
James's reign imprisoned
in the Tower of London.
A disastrous expedition to
the Orinoco in 1617
resulted in his execution
the following year.
Portrait by an
unknown artist.

BELOW Enamelled gold
badge of a Baronet of
Nova Scotia. In 1624 James
offered this new title to
certain supporters of
Sir William Alexander of
Menstrie's scheme for
founding a Scottish colony
between New England and
Newfoundland. Payment
of 6,000 marks or the
maintenance of six skilled
workmen as settlers for
two years secured a
baronetcy and 20,000
acres of land in
Nova Scotia.

James also took a keen interest in the short-lived foundation of Nova Scotia under Sir William Alexander – he who had aided the King with his translation of the Psalms. The history proper of the colony belongs to the next reign, but when Alexander's project failed, James himself did try to create an order of baronets of Nova Scotia, open to Scots. The colony, he thought, would be 'a good work, a royal work, and one good for the kingdom', words which could be taken as the motto for the brighter side of James's colonial interests. Over the East India Company, on the other hand, James's worst qualities were displayed; his laziness in conducting business, his favouritism, his incompetence with money, all these faults were at work in causing him to revoke charters and letters patent already granted, and otherwise break what should have been solemn royal promises.

Another apparently disastrous area of James's colonial policy was centred on Sir Walter Ralegh. The great adventurer was allowed out of prison in one last gambler's throw of a search for gold up the Orinoco; the expedition failed in every way, and since Ralegh had brushed with the Spaniards, James finally had him executed to appease them. There was much indignation at the time on the grounds that James was a puppet who had twitched to the machinations of the Spanish King, dictated by his Ambassador Gondomar. Recently it has been suggested that James at least did believe quite genuinely in the possibilities of the Orinoco venture, or at any rate believed that Ralegh would not attack San Thomé. This defends him from the charge of treachery, and leaves him having behaved weakly. But whether or not James was the tool of Gondomar, his attitude to Ralegh fits more properly into the pattern of his foreign policy than his colonial record.

James's pro-Spanish designs received lukewarm welcome from his fellow countrymen, in whom the need to fight the Spaniard had been ingrained since the days of Elizabeth. The death of Ralegh, which he met with characteristic constancy and courage, was considered at the time to be a lurid blot on James's reputation. His foreign policy, and in particular his reliance on the wily Spanish envoy, has received a tough press from many historians since, even though we no longer accept the notion that James was completely controlled by Gondomar. But James's feel for peace was in fact by far the soundest of his

political instincts. Like other ideas considered controversial in his own time, it is more acceptable to our own age than the bellicosity of those who surrounded him. One of King James's biographers, D. H. Willson, has called his foreign policy, his desire for universal peace, 'the most impossible of all his dreams'. That may be so. It is always difficult to know by what criterion a foreign policy should be judged afterwards. It is true that James was not successful in implementing his desires. On the other hand if the utilitarian standard of success is not too rigorously applied, James's dream was surely an honourable one.

For James believed passionately in peace both by temperament and by conviction. Gondomar attributed it rudely to his physical cowardice: 'fear alone guides the King'. The Tuscan resident put it more fairly: James was 'pacific by nature which many called timidity, as well as lenient, and averse to the shedding of blood'. But there was another side to it, expressed by James's own motto *Beati pacifici* – Blessed are the peacemakers. That was the concept of a Christian monarch, who believed that in peace rather than war the true glory of government was to be found. John Donne put the King's wishes in perspective, preaching in 1617, when he began by quoting: 'It is the Lord that hath done it, and it is wonderful in our eyes',

> ... that a King, born and bred in a warlike nation, and so accustomed to the sword, as that it had been directed upon his own person, in the strength of his age, and in his Infancy, in his Cradle, in his mother's belly should yet have the blessed spirit of peace so abundantly in him, as that by his Councils and his authority he should sheathe all the swords of Christendom again.

Nowadays, with the aid of psychology, we may suppose that it was just these early experiences which were responsible for breeding this spirit in James. But with Donne we can admire it.

Nothing demonstrates more clearly than the troubles of Charles I in foreign wars how right James had been in principle in his emphasis on peace. For one thing, the Anglo-Spanish treaty of 1604 left English trade free to develop, just as the colonies were founded. New enterprises flourished. The trouble was that James's theory of how peace might be maintained – a Spanish alliance combined with Protestant negotiations to balance it – aroused all the prejudices of the English against the alliance. The negotiations, on the other hand, provided no

SVPER·EST

RELIGIO.

PAX.

THE
WORKES
OF THE MOST HIGH
AND MIGHTY PRINCE,
IAMES,
By the grace of God, Kinge
of Great Brittaine
France & Ireland
Defendor of ỹ
Faith &c:
Published by IAMES, BISHOP of
WINTON & Deane of his
Mᵗⁱ Chappell Royall.
1 Reg: 3. 12. v. Loe I haue giuen thee
a wise and an vnderstanding heart.

LONDON
Printed by ROBERT
BARKER & Iohn Bill.
Printers to ỹ Kings mos t
excellent Maiestie.
1616.

Cum priuilegio.

Renold Elstrack sculpsit.

counter triumphs of Protestantism to make the national pulse beat faster. There were no victories to report in great speeches, no Tilburys, no Armadas defeated. And James did miss an opportunity in not leaning at first towards the Protestant Dutch – he could never quite forgive the United Provinces for their anti-monarchical views which had led them to throw off the Spanish yoke. In 1603 he had observed concerning the Spaniards and the Dutch that 'neither the condition of his own estate, neither the inclination of his mind, did permit him that for friendship of one he would enter into war with another, but that always he was resolved to carry an even hand betwixt them both'. Nevertheless in 1613 James offered to forge a defensive treaty with the princes of the German Protestant Union. In this alliance, cemented by the marriage of Princess Elizabeth, and his efforts to bring together Danes, Dutch and Swedes, James believed he had the right formula for peace, provided that the Spanish marriage of his heir offered a sufficient Catholic counterbalance.

The origins of the Thirty Years' War lay in a Protestant revolt in Bohemia against the Catholic and Habsburg King. The crown of Bohemia was then offered to James's son-in-law, the Elector Frederick of the Palatine, who assumed it in 1619. James now found himself in an unconscionably difficult position: the betting from the first was very strong that Catholic and Habsburg Spain would come to the aid of Austria. How could the Anglo-Spanish alliance, let alone the desired marriage of Prince Charles, be consummated in such circumstances, with the King's Protestant son-in-law in such peril? In fact for some time James continued to put the interests of peace, as he saw them, above those of family. When Frederick first assumed the Crown, he observed that 'his subjects were as dear to him as his children, and therefore he would not embark them in an unjust and needless quarrel'. James continued to draw close to Spain. He tried to ward off the threat of Spanish action against Frederick by making it clear that England would be absolutely obliged to fight if the Palatinate were touched. With the King so reluctant to desert his policy of peace, surely Spain would not push him to the point of no return.

In the meantime the national mood of England was very different. Prince Charles and his new comrade and ally Buckingham were breathing youthful fire and fury. And once Spain had signed a formal treaty with Austria to invade in February 1620, it was difficult to see how poor James could wriggle out of the martial gestures which he so much dreaded. His son-in-law and daughter were soon ejected, not only from their new acquisition of Bohemia, but also from the Palatinate which indubitably belonged to Frederick. In England, references to Queen Elizabeth grew apace and, rather like references to the spirit of Dunkirk in a modern national crisis, began to sound like clichés. The somewhat parsimonious and canny nature of the old Queen, who had certainly not believed in reckless European wars for glory's sake, was quite forgotten; Elizabeth seemed to stand for Protestant values which James, with his eternal Spanish hopes, was quite neglecting. How had Catholicism become so powerful in Europe that poor Protestant princes could be put out of doors by Catholic kings? As one tract put it a little later, 'some there are that find such fault with your Majesties government, as they wish Queen Elizabeth were alive again, who (they say) would never have suffered the enemies of her religion to have unbalanced Christendom, as they have done within these few years'.

The prospect of putting troops into Europe had one inevitable consequence for James, and it was one he could well have done without. A benevolence or appeal on behalf of the Palatinate raised some money (Prince Charles gave £10,000), but for real funds there was only one body who could help, and that was the long-neglected Parliament. As James himself said, in ten years he had not received a single subsidy, and that was 'a very long time to live like a shell-fish upon his own Moisture, without any public supply'. But it was hardly likely that the Parliament first assembled on 30 January 1621 would simply vote the required monies and leave it at that. The King opened Parliament with a long and rambling speech, in which he referred to himself as still treating for peace, albeit with a sword in his hand: he resented his financial dependence: 'I am to provide for wars . . .,' he said, 'and nothing can be expected of you without begging as a man would beg for alms.' Nevertheless he expressed the twin hopes that the members would 'make good laws but not to clog them with impertinences'.

In the event neither hope was fulfilled. The Commons,

outraged by the sort of financial expedients which had been employed in its absence, pounced on the royal policies. The granting of patents and monopolies to private persons constituted an outstanding grievance. Most of them involved control of some particular trade or industrial process. James found these grants to be an excellent method of rewarding his favourites, or even paying his own debts. In view of the justified indignation of the House of Commons, it was tragic that the prime favourite Buckingham and his family were so heavily involved in this murky trade. They controlled for example the licensing of inns, ale-houses, and the manufacturing of gold and silver thread. Wise Bacon, aware of what was coming, tried to warn Buckingham : 'Your Lordship (whom God hath made in all things so fit to be beloved),' he wrote, 'would put off the envy of these things (which I think in themselves bear no great fruit) and rather take the thanks for ceasing them, than the note for maintaining them.' But Buckingham was blind to the danger.

The Commons also insisted on discussing the King's pro-Spanish foreign policy, and the projected marriage of Charles – to James's absolute disgust, since foreign policy at least was unarguably part of the royal prerogative. But of course the raising of money was not. In the granting of subsidies, Parliament had its own historic role. In the sense that the two, foreign policy and financial supplies, had in this Parliament become inextricably entwined, James's assembly of 1621 prefigured all the later troubles of the Stuarts and their Parliaments. Historic precedent with regard to foreign policy was with James. But he would have been in a better position to continue that precedent free from interference, had he not been in desperate need of money on the one hand, and faced with a militantly Protestant House of Commons on the other.

As it was, the King's servant Bacon was sacrificed. In March he was impeached for taking bribes as Lord High Chancellor. Bacon's own excuse that he had been 'frail and partook of the abuse of the times' also sadly had a ring of truth. All the same he was fined £40,000 and put in prison from where he was subsequently released by the King's intervention.

As the year wore on, King and Commons proved to have irreconcilable differences. James desired to trust to the honour of the new King of Spain – Philip IV succeeded in 1621 – to restore

OPPOSITE Portrait of King James by Paul van Somer, c. 1620. In the background is the Whitehall Banqueting House, then under construction.

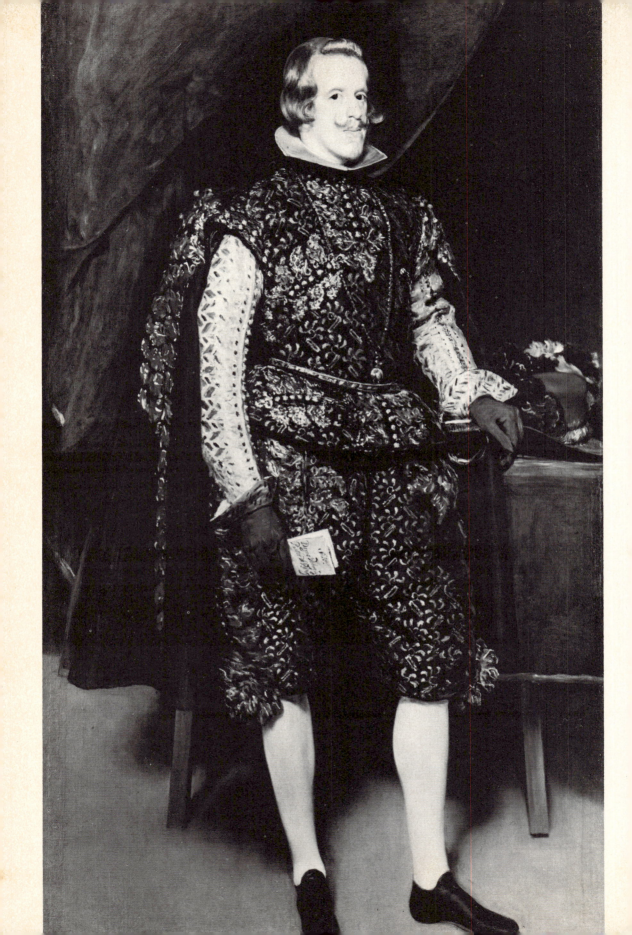

Frederick to the Palatinate. The Commons responded with protests against the prospect of a Spanish marriage and calls for Protestant action. James's irritation with this continued assault on the royal prerogative, as he saw it, was expressed by his greeting to a delegation of members received at Newmarket in December. 'Bring stools for the ambassadors,' he cried out crossly. Thus his third Parliament was dissolved in January 1622, and still no subsidy had been voted. James's justification for the dissolution began by stating that no justification was in fact necessary, since 'the assembling, continuing and dissolving of Parliaments be a prerogative so peculiarly belonging to our Imperial Crown ...'. Nevertheless, he went on to explain that certain members of Parliament had begun to discuss matters 'that were no fit subjects to be treated of in Parliament', as well as speaking disrespectfully of foreign princes. If the Commons' interpretation of their own rights had been accepted, James's own 'inseparable rights' and prerogative, 'annexed to our Imperial crown', would have been fatally impaired. On this gloomy note of warning a moneyless James returned to grapple with the problems of unbalanced Christendom, without the benefit of his awkward Commons.

OPPOSITE Philip IV, King of Spain; portrait by Velasquez.

8
Continual
Cares

Look not to find the softness of a down pillow in a crown, but remember that it is a thorny piece of stuff and full of continual cares.

From King James's *Meditations on St Matthew*

IN 1620 KING JAMES had published a small book of meditations on verses 27 to 29 of the twenty-seventh chapter of *St Matthew*, that passage relating to the Passion of Jesus where he was stripped of his garments and crowned with a wreath of thorns. The King drew a gloomy parallel with the fate of earthly monarchs: 'Look not to find the softness of a down pillow in a crown,' he wrote, 'but remember that it is a thorny piece of stuff and full of continual cares.' The remaining years of his life certainly justified this sad estimate. Not only was he ageing, sick and unhappy, but he was confronted increasingly with the shrewish coalition of Prince Charles and Buckingham. Sometimes they treated him as if they had been two sharp-tongued young wives managing a doddery old husband. In addition to all her other advantages, how fortunate if selfish had been the late Virgin Queen in her lack of heirs! It was fortune that she had merited, since she had made such a feature of avoiding the rising sun. James, having performed the more altruistic duty of a sovereign, if the dynasty was to survive at all, and provided heirs, endured all the consequent problems. Prince Charles, as even Prince Henry had done before his early death, provided a natural focus for policies in opposition to the King's own.

At the same time, James's failing powers were the subject of frequent public comment: in February 1623 the Venetian Ambassador described his reluctance to give audiences and his 'lethal sickness'. All good sentiments were clearly dead in the King. He was blinded by disordered self-love and his wish for quiet and pleasure. Agitated by constant mistrust of everyone, tyrannised over by perpetual fear for his life, James nevertheless managed to be 'tenacious of his authority as against Parliament and jealous of the prince's obedience'. The Ambassador painted a cruel picture of senility. In fact the ageing process of King James was still capable of intermittent remission. However debilitated the King might be, he still had a far better head on his shoulders than either Charles or Buckingham; while a recent detailed study of the Parliament of 1624 reveals that he was still capable of flashes of his old Scottish shrewdness.

The dangerous rashness of the Charles–Buckingham combination was revealed by their foolish expedition to Spain early in 1623 to woo the Infanta. It was true that James had set his heart on the completion of the European balancing-act

contained in a Spanish Catholic marriage for his son. But his
embarrassments towards the Palatinate were by no means
solved, and the King wisely sought relief from commitment in a
policy of procrastination. His daughter Elizabeth, to some the
Queen of Hearts but to others the Helen of Germany for the
troubles she had sparked off, wrote in vain to James:

> Your Majesty will understand by the king's letters how the
> Palatinate is in danger of being utterly lost if your majesty gives us
> not some aid. I am sorry we are obliged to trouble your majesty so
> much with our affairs, but their urgency is so great that we cannot
> do otherwise.

She was merely adjured by the British Ambassador to remember the pious resignation of 'our last, eternally glorious
Elizabeth'.

By January 1623, James still hoped to avoid coming to any
decision on the subject of war on behalf of the Elector's
inherited territory. At the same time he signed the articles of
marriage with Spain, including a private letter which promised
to give alleviation to the English Catholics from the penal laws
of the country, so long as they did not give public scandal. As
for the Palatinate, James's plan was that it should be sequestered
in the hands of the Infanta. It was at this point that Charles and
Buckingham, who had been invited by the departing Gondomar
to prosecute the Prince's suit in person, decided to set out for
Madrid. James was extraordinarily reluctant to give his assent,
and rightly so. His reluctance was due not only to his love of the
two young men, but also to sheer common sense. It was not by
that sort of impetuous action, when young, that James had
hung on to his sovereignty in Scotland. But now he was old and
without strength, crippled with arthritis, the victim of the
pressing energy of the rising generation. 'The King seems
practically lost,' wrote one observer. 'He now protests, now
weeps, but finally gives in.' There is another glimpse of him
'demanding only repose, and, indeed, the tomb'.

In vain James attempted to put a good gloss on it all, by
reminding the world, in a poem, that many of Charles's forbears had sought their spouses abroad:

> So Jack and Tom do nothing new
> When love and fortune they pursue. . . .

Weldon for once had justice on his side when he denounced the

202

THE SPANISHE PARL'AMENT.

Ingentibus exidit ausis.

'folly of this voyage, plotted only by green heads'. As Bishop
Goodman said, it was James's 'old wits and kingcraft which saw
the dangers' of which the green heads were blissfully – or wil-
fully – unaware. As James raised Buckingham to a dukedom in
his absence, and made preparations for the fleet which would
bring back the Infanta, he had time to bemoan the chapel built
for her anticipated devotions in England : 'We are building a
temple to the devil', said the King.

When the news came in June that the Spanish wanted Charles
to spend another year in Spain, James broke down and wrote a
series of frantic letters to his 'sweet boys' to come home, unless
they were prepared never to see their 'old dad' again. James
wore a portrait of 'Steenie' – Buckingham – in a blue ribbon
under his waistcoat next to his heart. His anguished appeals
still have the power to move one, with their mixture of pathos
and the absurd :

> Alas, I now repent me sore that I ever suffered you to go away,
> I care for match nor nothing, so I may once have you in my arms
> again; God grant it! God grant it! Amen, amen, amen ... God
> bless you both, my only sweet son and my only best sweet servant
> and God send you a happy and joyful meeting in the arms of your
> dear old dad.

The sweet boys, however, were obdurate where the old dad
was not. And Steenie wrote back impudent letters, asking for
jewels and ending, 'I kiss your dirty hands.' So the jewels went
off, and in July the chastened old dad signed much improved
articles from the Spanish point of view : public articles allowed
the Infanta to worship in a church open not only to Spaniards
but to the English as well (a revolutionary concept by the
standards of the time), while secret ones referred again to the
lifting of the penalties against the English Catholics. It was,
incidentally, in the course of these negotiations that the English
Catholic body first became known officially as *Roman* Catholics :
for the Spanish, knowing that the Church of England also
regarded itself as the Catholic Church, insisted on the insertion
of the word. Still James, for all his loneliness, had not quite lost
his cunning. He did tell the Spanish Ambassadors that he would
cancel these concessions, if affairs of State demanded it.

Finally Charles himself was brought to realise the humiliation
which he had sought in the Spanish expedition. His bride – with

her desirable dowry of £600,000 – was not going to be allowed to leave Spain. The Spaniards had been temporising, as James had temporised over the Palatinate. Buckingham and Charles returned in October. They now sang a very different tune. The King, they said, should now declare war on Spain. Still James would not commit himself. But he was at least obliged to summon Parliament, which he opened in February 1624. Once again this Parliament was marked by a lack of royal management, based on insufficient organisation. And there was a further awkwardness, in that the six Privy Councillors still in the Commons, who might have directed matters for James, found affairs taken out of their hands by Charles and Buckingham. Furthermore, there was a basic divergence between James and the two young men over what they hoped that this Parliament would produce. James expected a series of aggressive speeches from the Members which would strengthen his own hand in negotiations; he would thus be able to extort much better conditions for the restitution of Frederick and Elizabeth to the Palatinate, and all within a peaceful context. Charles and

James welcoming his son Charles home after his expedition to Spain to woo the Infanta.

Buckingham were not so subtle. Quite simply, they wanted this Parliament to finance a war against Spain.

King James, for all his declining years and continuous cares, played his hand skilfully with the Spanish envoys, as the analysis of this Parliament by Robert L. Ruigh shows. While continuing to badger the Spaniards on the subject of the Palatinate, James also used concessions to Parliament to apply added pressure. His aim was to demonstrate that the will of the King was their only protection against an outright declaration of war. James, of course, was setting a dangerous precedent in thus permitting Parliament to discuss foreign policy, hitherto the acknowledged preserve of the royal prerogative: his violent explosions on the subject during the previous session will be recalled. His excuse was that Parliament's role remained consultative rather than mandatory. And that was true enough. For throughout the session, James refused to consider declaring war against Spain, except for the specific purpose of securing the return of the Palatinate. When the Commons declined to allow this proviso to be entered into the bill for subsidies, the King asserted his right to alter it 'and set his marginal note upon it'. James was surely right in trying to avoid an out and out Spanish war, not only on grounds of expense, but also of practicality. It would be far easier to rescue the Palatinate if Spain held off from interference.

There were now plans to marry off Charles to a French Princess, Henrietta Maria, sister of Louis XIII. At first, both King and Prince vowed that in this case the Catholics in England would not receive toleration, but by November, secret clauses concerning the Catholics had crept into the marriage treaty on the insistence of Cardinal Richelieu. It was as well that Parliament had been prorogued at the end of May for there would have been an outcry; as it was, James had to break his promise for a new session in the autumn, for fear of violent objections to such leniency. The expedition of British troops to Europe in the following year to rescue the Palatinate, can only have confirmed all the failing King's gloomiest fears about military commitment. Money was tight. An expedition against Cadiz failed. The Huguenots were not relieved at La Rochelle – 'Since England was England she received not so dishonourable a blow,' wrote Denzil Holles, one of the more extreme of the Parliamentary

OPPOSITE Charles as Prince of Wales; portrait by Daniel Mytens.

207

Puritans. As Buckingham had led the La Rochelle disaster, one bitter wit contrasted the favourite's prowess with the hero of the last reign : 'Send forth your Drakes and keep at home your Duke.' And James refused to let the expedition go to the relief of the Dutch fortress of Breda, which was being besieged by Spain, for all the insistence of the French.

While James angled in vain to save the Palatinate and, at the same time, preserve peace, his country was in the throes of other difficulties which owed nothing to the claims of foreign policy. For the economic blight of the times King James was scarcely responsible. Unfortunately the Great Depression of the 1620s, as R. H. Tawney has pointed out, was a political as well as an economic event. 'All grievances in the kingdom are trifles compared with the decay of trade', was one judgment; 'poverty and want pinch the kingdom', was another. It was regrettable that James did not cease his flow of golden disbursements as he grew older ; rearmament and diplomatic activity all devoured money; as for expensive little details, like Charles's journey to Spain and the fleet standing at the ready for his return, it was understandable that Cranfield was said to be 'sick at heart with these extraordinary charges'. Worst of all, the phenomenon of rapidly rising prices vitiated the economic climate still further.

It was unfortunate that Cranfield (now Earl of Middlesex), who had done so much to act as the saviour of the royal finances and now vainly suggested cuts in the pension bill, was not personally impregnable. His competence with money was matched with a less useful gift for making enemies, amongst them Buckingham, who had hoped to find in Cranfield a source of funds, and had been disappointed. In May 1624, Cranfield was successfully impeached by the Commons, for 'bribery, extortion, oppression, wrong and deceipts' : the actual cause of his fall was a mere pretext – the imposition on certain wines into London and groceries in the provinces. But the measure met with the enthusiastic approval of Charles and Buckingham. King James was left to comment on the incident that Charles would live to have his bellyful of Parliaments ; as for Steenie, he was a fool and was making a rod with which to scourge himself – two melancholy but accurate predictions. Although the fall of Cranfield moves us less than that of Wolsey – the man

Theobalds, James's country house twelve miles north of London, which he acquired in 1607 in exchange for Hatfield, and where he died on 27 March 1625. Drawing by John Thorpe.

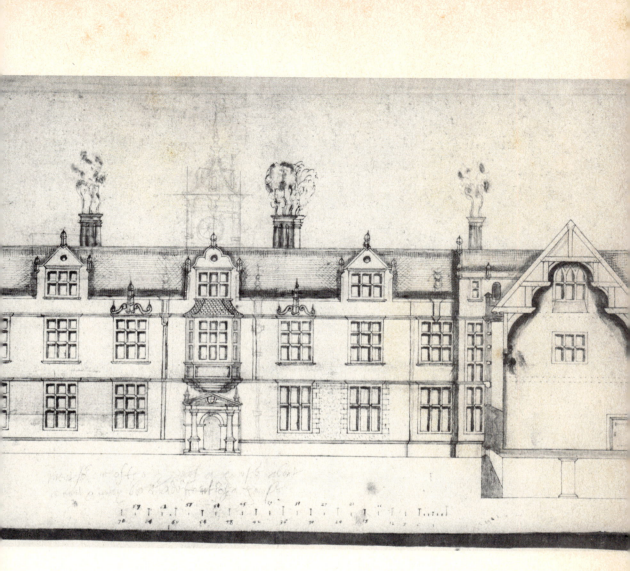

was not so epic, his works not so fine and his end not so tragic – at least the financier like the Cardinal could say that he had served his King diligently, or, in the words of John Eliot, he had 'done him that service that few had ever done'.

On 5 March 1625 King James fell sick following a hunting expedition at Theobalds of what was described as 'as ordinary and moderate tertian ague' – a type of fever common in a pre-antibiotic age, so called because its course followed a three-day cycle. But he did not recover as was expected. James collapsed suddenly – possibly with the type of convulsion common to porphyria, or from a stroke – and ended his days speechless, without the doctors being able to hold out any hope. Bucking-ham and his mother, distraught that the royal physicians were

Design by Inigo Jones
for the catafalque
of King James.

failing so signally in their treatment, tried some 'country'
remedies, of the type which would now be described as homeo-
pathic. Later these innocent attempts to save James were trans-
formed into deliberate attempts to poison him. Sir Anthony
Weldon, vilifier of the Stuarts, made the most of the accusation.
James, he said, was given black plaster and powder by Buckingham and so died. A servant was said to have protested to the
favourite: 'Ah, my lord, you have undone us, all his poor
servants, altho' you are so well provided you need not care.' At
this Buckingham rushed to the King's bedside: 'Justice, sir, I am
abused by your servant and wrongfully accused.' But the King
fixed his mournful eyes upon him as one who would have said
'Not wrongfully.' As late as the trial of Charles I, the charge of
causing his father's death by poison in association with Buckingham was still brought up against him.

Nothing as dramatic as poison marked the deathbed of King

James. The truth was that his physician Sir William Paddy, coming down to Theobalds, quickly perceived that there was nothing to be done for him but pray for his soul. This the Bishop of Lincoln did, while the poor King, weakened by the unpleasant demands of dysentery, lay speechless, robbed of his dignity even in death. The kindest version of his deathbed suggested that his eyes, 'the messengers of his heart', were lifted to heaven at the end of every prayer, even though he could no longer even say Amen. James VI and I died on 27 March 1625, in his fifty-ninth year. The details of his autopsy sound curiously appropriate: all the vitals were sound, as also was his head, which was very full of brains; but his blood was wonderfully tainted with melancholy. So his continual cares were over.

James's State funeral would however have been after his own heart: for like his son's Banqueting House, it embodied those principles of kingship in which he believed so passionately, but had been constantly restricted from putting into practice. His catafalque was designed by Inigo Jones. First of all John Donne preached over his corpse at Denmark House. Then the actual funeral was held in Westminster Abbey. There, for 250 years, the precise position of his body went unrecorded until the great Victorian Dean Stanley instituted a search. He found the body of King James in the tomb of Henry VII. It was fully in keeping with James's aspirations that he should have chosen to lie with another sovereign who had founded a dynasty, the first Stuart thus keeping company for eternity with the first Tudor. The total cost of the funeral was enormous, rumoured to be over £50,000. But there would not be another such magnificent display of mourning for a quarter of a century, in fact not until the obsequies of Oliver Cromwell in 1658: bewilderingly enough, for want of another model, these were founded on the ceremonial usage for James, catafalque included.

The whole drama of the English Civil War lay between those two similar and splendid burials. Nevertheless the retrospective shadow of our most fascinating contest should not blind us to the many virtues of King James. His reputation provides a classic example of the evil which men do living after them, and the good being oft interred in the grave. Against his extravagance, which is not to be denied, should be put the stark poverty of his Scottish condition which does at least explain it; and it is certainly unfair, although it has been done, to complain at the same time that he did not keep up the state of a monarch. It should be remembered that James inherited from his great predecessor a burden of debts and a most inadequate financial system: as for his lordly subjects who kept such state around him, from the industrious Cecil to Suffolk the family man, they were living off the back of the King, and not always with permission to do so.

James's laziness in his later years over the conduct of business, and his preference for country life and hunting, is a fault which has been generally condemned. Yet very often it was his masterly inactivity, as one authority has termed it, which brought the best results. He had also inherited a sour and aggressive House of Commons: the gossamer skeins of the royal prerogative were somehow preserved from their grasping fingers until the end of the reign. James did not leave all his political cunning behind him in Scotland. The activism of King Charles I had far more disastrous results. As for James's love of peace, which Bishop Goodman dwelt on at length in his funeral sermon, that had the added advantage of being consonant with his limited financial resources. Bold, swashbuckling campaigns might suit the national mood of nostalgia for Elizabeth's reign, but they had a habit of costing money, and money James simply did not have.

James's Scottish training, as well as his Scottish success, has been stressed in the present narrative, not only because it helps to explain what sort of man ascended the British throne, but also because it enabled James to think of Britain as a coherent geographical entity: it has always been notoriously easier to do that from the vantage point of Edinburgh than that of London. James's concept of Great Britain was one contribution. His own learning and appreciation of it in others, his interest in divinity and teaching, epitomised by the commissioning of the King James' Bible, must be rated another. In later years, James's concentration on his favourites, particularly as he himself degenerated physically, should not distract one from the extension of their own rights claimed by the Commons. It is true that these rights have been won long since, and happily so: James's own theory of the royal prerogative sounds highly pretentious by modern standards. But these are not the standards

OPPOSITE Akbar, Mogul Emperor of India, receiving gifts from princes of different nations, one of whom is thought to be King James; seventeenth-century Mogul drawing.

212

OPPOSITE Broadside
lamenting the death of
King James.

which should ever be applied to the early seventeenth century.
James was fair in his opinion that some of the privileges claimed
by the Commons were not historically justified.

Above all, James fell under that cloud which falls athwart a
country when the great sun goes in: the sun in this case was
Queen Elizabeth. It is her golden memory, sometimes much
exaggerated, which often prevents justice being done to the
memory of James, as he suffered from it in his own lifetime. Let
us assess James by his own sonnet at the start of *Basilikon Doron*,
when he laid down the precepts for a King:

> God gives not Kings the style of Gods in vain,
> For on his throne his Sceptre do they sway:
> And as their subjects ought them to obey,
> So Kings should fear and serve their God again.

Perhaps James did not have the style of a God, and erred in
thinking that it had been granted to him. Nor did he create it for
himself as Elizabeth had created the style of a Goddess. But he
did fear God and attempt to serve Him by his own lights. As a
result, his subjects, even if they did not always obey him, were
not so badly served by him after all.

A FVNERAL ELEGIE VPON

The lamentable losse of our late Leige and Royall King IAMES departed.

Anno Dom. 1625.
March 27.

WHo can induce his mournfull Muse to (sing
The Exequies of our deceased King?
But he shall finde his minde with Griefe
To pen a Poem, or to publish it, (vnfit
Such quelling force, hath sad-vnlookt-for newes
Over the Soule, as that it doth infuse
Nothing but dolors, and doth cause the brest
To be with dismall Lethargies opprest,
So that awhile hauing receiu'd griefes Wound,
We seeme dead-smitten to the dampish ground,
And by much sorrow senselesse are, so that
Weery, and sometimes haue forgot for what:
And he that would a solid Verse compose,
Must banish from him intellectuall foes,
Such as are sorrowes, and disastrous Passions,
Sad Humors, Rumors, inward perturbations,
Distracting Terrors, Errors bread by Fame,
When lying flying tales peruert the same;
And feare lest these should intermingle Veritie,
Makes the heart dumpish, and mistrusts Sinceritie.
And there is none, who is a Subiect true,
That can so soone to sorrow say adiew,
Whose verie soule is not as yet perplext,
Disquieted, turmoyl'd, and foyl'd, and vext,
When he remembers (oh! I sigh to tell)
King Iames his bidding to this life farewell;
Then blame ye not my rugged, ragged Rimes,
O ye, the Nectar-Poets of our times;
Halfe sentences, sad words, hath Tunes and Tones,
Best testifie the passionatest moanes;
The Sacred-Frenzie, and the sugred straines,
I now bequeath vnto more happie Veines:
For if I euer had a Faculty
Of Versifying, it from me did fly,
When as this wofull voice was vttered,
The mightie Monarch Iames is lately dead.
That now my heart can onely pant, and throbs
Speaking imperfect sounds, cut off by sobs
A KING is gone, who for his Wisdomes store,
England did neuer shew the like before;
In Poetrie he likewise did excell,
And Oratorie as the World can tell;
For diuers volumes learnedly he writ,
Stuft with deepe Art, and Quintissence of wit.

All Graces in his Heart did spring and breed,
In Science, Conscience, he did exceed,
And in his praise some Poet did indite
This Distticke, which I vnderneath will write;
For Wisdome Salomon, Dauid for Pietie,
An heau'nly Man, if not an earthly Deitie.
His Gracious Spirits did in one combine
To make iust Lawes, both Morall and Diuine,
He did inuent and vent marks to descrie
The colour'd shewes of Romes Idolatrie:
He pull'd the maske from off that Skarlet Whore,
And made her better knowne than ere before,
That all the Kings which liue vpon this Round,
May Romish Babel studie to confound.
He sought against her with that mightie Sword,
Gods euerlasting vndiminisht Word.
And now may those, who wish Romes ouerthrow
(He gaue the onset) strike the second blow.
It was enough for him that he des'd her,
And by his writings publiquely descri'd her:
He shew'd that Enemie, which once must fall,
Happie be they which shall breake downe her wall.
Me thinkes I see his bookes taking their leaue
Of him, from whom they Being did receiue,
And heare his Soule speaking, as it was flying,
Being about to leaue his bodie dying,
Farewell my works, but may est thou neuer die,
Which doest detect Papall Apostasie;
Be thou the Summoner to cause Romes harmes;
Fill Realmes with these, or some such like Alarmes,
Arise ye Monarchs, looke you, this is she,
'Gainst whom your forces should conuerted be:
Pull downe her Tripple Crowne, settle vpon her,
Depriue her of her glorie and her honour.
Why to your selues doe you inferre a wound?
Ioynt-forces ruinate her to the ground.
Why doe you liue amongst your selues at iarres?
Weakening your powers by your Ciuill warres:
Consent, for you are brethren, agree;
Ye all of Rome must ioynt Destroyers bee.
Why should Manasses eat vp Ephraim,
And Ephraim, Manasses; Ioyne with him,
The Lord of Hosts, who saith Babel shall fall;
Be ye his Instruments to pull downe all.

I who am dying had determination,
To haue procur'd this foretold Desolation;
And therefore did endeuour to keepe peace,
That ciuill warres amongst our selues should cease:
But Heauens did not allot me so great Fame
To supplant Rome, though I had such a name;
For I must die, my time is come, glasse runne,
The Cloud of death must hide my shining Sunne.
Rome may perhaps reioyce, and triumphs keepe,
When she shall heare that I am falne asleepe,
I'th' morning of my warres; but let her know
Her Trophees doe before her troubles goe.
My hands I sacrifice free from warres staine,
Vnto that Lord who menaceth her paine.
Open ye Heauens, and doe my soule inuest,
Wars are begun on earth, but let me rest.
And now, dread King, I greeue that thou art dead,
And yet reioyce that thou art gathered
Vnto thy Fathers in Celestiall Peace;
For from contending cares thy brest shall cease.
And I reioyce there sits vpon thy Throne,
The liuing Picture of dead Salomon,
Castor did set, and both his lights did close,
But Pollux, or Apollo soone arose;
Who shall protect these lands safe round about,
And guide their goings in and commings out.
Whom Moses-like the Lord from waues did free,
And made him Ruler, England, ouer thee:
He did refuse to be of Pharaohs kin,
And yeelded not to their blasphemous sin,
Whose Crowne vpon his head the Lord keepe sure,
As long as shall the Sun and Moone endure.
Amen.

FINIS.

London, Printed for Iohn Wright.

Select bibliography

Some recent books on King James

King James VI and I, D. H. Willson, Bedford Historical Series, 1956.
An all-round biography.

King James I, David Mathew, 1967.
Recommended for its study of the King's literary works.

James I by his contemporaries, Robert Ashton, 1969.
Well-edited compendium of original sources.

The Making of a King, Caroline Bingham, 1969.
The childhood and youth of James put into perspective.

The Reign of James VI and I, edited by Alan G. R. Smith, Problems in Focus, 1973.
Studies, based on up-to-date scholarship, of a variety of aspects of the King's reign.

Acknowledgments

Photographs and illustrations are supplied by or reproduced by kind permission of the following:

By gracious permission of Her Majesty The Queen: 10–11, *15, 38,* 96 *(above), 161,* 170, 171, 174, 179, 180, 181, 183, 184–5, 186 *(above),* 191, 194, 203, 206

By courtesy of His Grace the Duke of Atholl (photo Tom Scott): 45

From the Woburn Abbey Collection, by kind permission of His Grace, the Duke of Bedford: 54

British Museum: 33, 35, 37, 48, 51, 56 *(below),* 68, *84,* 90–91, 92, 95, 98, 100, 106 *(above),* 130, 142, 143 *(right and left below),* 148, 154, 158, 159 *(below),* 162, 166–7

Collection of R. H. Davies (photo Courtauld Institute): 121

Devonshire Collection, Chatsworth. Reproduced by permission of the Trustees of the Chatsworth Settlement: 122, *132*

Edinburgh Public Libraries: 147

Edinburgh University Library: *141 (below)*

Department of the Environment: 13, 19, *176* (Crown Copyright: reproduced by permission of the Controller of Her Majesty's Stationery Office)

By courtesy of Mr Stewart Fotheringham: 43

Freer Gallery of Art, Washington D.C.: 213

Glasgow University: 56 *(above)*

Mansell Collection: 50, 136–7

Mary Evans Picture Library: 135, 159 *(above),* 186 *(below)*

Methuen Collection, Corsham Court, Wiltshire: 79

By courtesy of J. R. More-Molyneux: *93*

National Gallery: 196

National Gallery of Ireland, Dublin: 87

National Monuments Records of Scotland, Crown Copyright: reproduced by permission of the Controller of Her Majesty's Stationery Office: 59

National Museum of Antiquities of Scotland: 61, 76, 188

National Portrait Gallery: *14,* 60, 88, 106 *(below),* 120, *141 (above),* 151, 153, *173,* 189

National Trust for Scotland: 71

North Carolina Museum of Art, Raleigh, N.C.: 138

Index

221

Comitum, Baronum, ac totius ordinis equestris cœlestis

Palatium regium
40 Trabanten.

...minē negst folgende

Anna Danica, Regina Ang: etc.

Chor des herlichen tempels so der West münster genant.

Iacobus D. gr Britannicarū Insularū rex

Cantuariensis et Eboracensis Archiepiscopi ducētes Regem. *Tres gladij prælati.* *Tuba...*